Ready, Set, Read: Reading Program

Vera Clark, M.A.

First Edition

Ready, Set, Read: Reading Program

By Vera Clark, M.A.

Published by: Dog Ear Publishing

First Printing 2010
Original Title (2009): *Vera Clark's Teach Me To Read English In 100 Easy Lessons*

Cover Design: SunUp Group, Inc.
Flash card animals: Rita Pacheco
Interior design: Lisa Liddy, The Printed Page
Lesson drawings and design: John Stone

Library of Congress Control Number: Applied for

Ready, Set, Read: Reading Program

ISBN: 978-160844-669-8

Printed in the United States of America

Dedication

To April, Carolyn, Katie and Eric,

Your eagerness to learn made the experience of teaching you to read a wonderful journey.

Disclaimer

We cannot guarantee that any person will learn to read with this reading program although the program is designed based upon the author's years of experience successfully teaching people how to read. If you are not satisfied with the reading program or have other concerns about the program please be aware that your sole remedy is to return the book, subject to the return policy where you purchased the book. We greatly value your input and feedback. We encourage you to send your comments, questions, and success stories to info@ReadySetReadNow.com.

Acknowledgments

I would like to recognize the people who have had the biggest impact on my life and my life's work. First of all, I want to thank my parents, CAPT Stanford E. Linzey, Jr., CHC USN (Ret.) and Verna M. Linzey, for their words of wisdom, common sense and support. I want to thank a wonderful man, Mr. Raymond Schiek, who was the first principal who hired me and believed in me as a teacher. His encouragement changed the course of my life. My beloved brothers and sisters: Gena, Janice, Eugene, Darnelle, Sharon, George, Paul, David and especially Jim, have taught and blessed me more than they know. In the early stage with the first draft, dear friends Juanita Price and Jenny Hughes gave many hours to proof-reading and giving helpful suggestions. I have been blessed to have friends and artists John Stone and Rita Pacheco, whose beautiful artwork and illustrations brought life and beauty to this work. My daughter, Katie, was always encouraging and helpful to me with her computer skills, and my son, Eric, offered comic relief whether I needed it or not! My daughters, April Moore, M.A. and Carolyn Dillinger, J.D. are the wonderful editors who spent hours to clarify, correct, cross-reference and fine-tune this reading program. These ladies are truly amazing. They inspired me to write this reading program, encouraged me throughout the process, and were here to the end putting on the final touches. To all of you I want to say "Thank you, and I love you."

Additional Ready, Set, Read Resources

Supplement your reading program with additional high-quality resources designed to make reading fun and easy for all ages and learners. Check our website www.readysetreadnow.com for these products and more.

Ready, Set, Read – on DVD

Ready, Set, Read is excited to announce *Ready, Set, Read* on DVD in which Vera Clark teaches Step 1, Step 2, and Step 3, including all 100 lessons. An amazing tool, the set of DVDs will help persons of any age who cannot read well, or at all, to learn to read by watching the DVDs, without the need of an outside teacher or tutor. Individuals or classrooms may wish to use this format as the primary teaching tool or as extra practice. This teaching format can be used on a television screen, personal DVD player, or in reading centers at computers.

Illustrated Lessons

Ready, Set, Read is proud to present the first 20 reading lessons in individual, full-color, illustrated children's books. These books are specifically designed, based on parent request, to hold a young child's attention with colors and pictures. These beautiful books will be sold in sets of five lessons.

Leveled Readers

Ready, Set, Read is busy at work producing leveled readers to supplement the basic reading program. After completion of lessons 1-5, and after every five lessons thereafter, supplemental leveled readers provide stories appropriately matched with the reading vocabulary learned up to that point.

Teacher's Kit

Ready, Set, Read is producing a Teacher's Kit to support teachers' use of the reading program in the classroom. The kit is available in a kit and on CD with the following items: Reading Lessons 1-100, Flash Cards in regular and classroom sizes, Success Charts, ABC Sound List, Wall ABC Charts, Phonics Progress Charts, and Pre-Kindergarten Reading Assessments.

About The Author

Vera is the seventh of ten children, born to Stanford and Verna Linzey, a Navy Captain/Chaplain and a homemaker, in San Diego, California. Being a Navy family, they moved to different parts of the country every couple of years. Vera graduated from Vanguard University of Southern California in Costa Mesa, California, with a Bachelor of Arts degree in Psychology and earned a Master of Arts degree in Education, with an emphasis in Special Education, from California State Polytechnic University in Pomona, California.

Vera is the mother of four children, and she has two grandchildren. Her first daughter, April Moore, is an assistant principal of a public high school and is presently working on a doctoral degree from USC. Vera's second daughter, Carolyn Dillinger, is a business attorney in Laguna Hills, California. Her third daughter Katie Waisanen, is a sophomore in college, and her son, Eric Waisanen, is a junior in high school. Vera lives in Southern California with her two youngest children.

Vera started teaching school in 1974, and quickly developed a strong interest in the subject of how we teach people to read. She felt that this subject was made to be far more difficult than necessary. Vera experimented with her own children, beginning when they were babies, and found that each child learned to read easily and was eager to do so. She continued studying and experimenting, refining and simplifying the process and taught adults as well as many children to read. Vera has taught in private and public schools, has home schooled, has taught children who were advanced as well as children with learning disabilities.

This reading program was written at the urging of her older daughters who recognized that their academic ease and success was credited to the ability to read at an early age. They wanted to give the same advantage to their children someday, therefore they asked Mom to carefully write down the process for them. Vera worked on this labor of love for six years, and incorporated the treasure of knowledge she gained in her thirty-plus years of teaching and parenting experience. Vera is a frequent speaker for educator and parent conferences.

Illustrators

John Stone

John Stone has done a wide variety of creative design. John has designed artificial limbs for amputees, has models of a space shuttle in the Kennedy Space Center, the Smithsonian and the James Bond Movie, *Moonraker.*

As a young child he had dreams of working for Disney as an artist. His opportunity came when Epcot Center was being developed, and he stepped into a position at Walt Disney Imagineering. He became intimately involved in the design of Journey into Imagination, The Land Pavilion and Transportation. While back in California he had full design control of Splash Mountain. As head Creative Designer, he also designed the Indiana Jones ride and the Many Adventures of Winnie the Pooh. His career at Disney as an Imagineer spanned 26 years.

After leaving Disney he illustrated children's books and designed sets for expos. John is an accomplished Architectural and Landscape Designer. He is supported at home by his wife, Debbie, who helps run their company, JS & Associates, Inc. He also has three daughters, Abigail, and twins Emily and Kelsie, who are following in their father's artistic footsteps. Contact him at Icandraw4u@ca.rr.com.

Rita Pacheco

Rita Pacheco attended Art Center college of Design in Pasadena, where she majored in illustration. During her career as an interior designer and illustrator, she created perspective renderings in water color for clients which included popular restaurants and hotels.

In 1993, after ten years in commercial art, Rita began her second career as a freelance fine artist. Her portfolio includes business and residential murals in acrylics; portraits from photographs and live subjects in pen-and-ink, water color, acrylics and oil, and landscape paintings in oil. Her work was honored with a First Place award for Event Design at the 2001 Fiesta de la Familia sponsored by the Press Enterprise in Riverside. She has generously donated her time and artistic talents to the Temescal Canyon High School Drama Department in Lake Elsinore, Cornerstone Community Church in Wildomar, the Ojai Raptor Center, and the Los Angeles City Fire Department.

Rita is a member of the Riverside Art Museum, the Plein Air Artists of Riverside, Fallbrook Art Association, and the Laguna Plein Air Painters Association. Visit her website at www.ritapacheco.com.

Table of Contents

Introduction

The purpose of this book is to show you how to teach someone to read. Teaching someone to read is really quite simple, when you have a plan. I have made that plan for you (see **Here's the Plan: As Easy as 1, 2, 3**). Anyone can do it, and that means you can too. Everything you need is right here.

Many parents have told me, "I would love to teach my child to read if I just knew what to do!" There are many different reading programs out there to help teach reading. Some of these are fine and can work if you use them consistently. The problem is that some programs are too complicated, too expensive, not thorough, or take too much time. Parents need an easy way to teach their children to read. My program is simple, inexpensive, thorough, easy-to-use, and has proven results.

I have been an educator for over thirty years, teaching in private schools, public schools and have homeschooled my own children. I have taught special education, regular education, English language learners, students who are educationally challenged, as well as students who are gifted. The most exciting and fulfilling teaching I have ever done is teaching my children how to read at home when they were very young.

I have four children, three daughters and one son. Before each child was one year old, I started teaching them the ABC's, using flash cards. By the time they were 3 years old, they were reading at a first grade level. This ability to read at a young age gave the children an advantage in all subject areas. School work was easy and fun. They were self-confident and had high self-esteem. These children loved reading and learning, therefore they continually wanted to learn more.

The ripple effect of early reading has continued into adult years for the older children. Each of the older daughters went off to a private university at 16 years of age. One was teaching at that university at 20 years of age, and now is an assistant principal of a public high school and working on a doctoral degree at USC. The other passed the California Bar Exam and was licensed as an attorney at 22 years of age; she is a business attorney with her own law practice. The younger daughter and son are teenagers and have each excelled in academics and are on an advanced pace.

I firmly believe that if a loving person spends the time and effort to teach a child to read, it will start the chain of events that will cause the child to be more intelligent than she or he would have been otherwise. It does not matter whether you are educated or not. It does not matter whether you consider yourself smart or not. What does matter is that you care enough for your child to take the time to teach her or him. It only takes about fifteen minutes a day.

A few years ago my older daughters asked me to write this book. They told me that when they have children, they want to teach them how to read just as I taught them. They wanted a step-by-step program to follow. This program is my life's work. My daughter is now using it to teach her two year old son, and he is on Lesson 1. Her ten month old daughter is learning the names and sounds of the letters.

I wrote this book for them and am now offering it to you. Bless your child and teach him or her to read. Teach a friend to read. Teach a homeless person to read. I have done these things and found it to be very rewarding to make a major difference in someone's life. The ripple effect of blessings continue forever and will bless you too. I will show you how to teach someone to read, and I will make it simple.

Enjoy the adventure!

God Bless You,
Vera Clark

Benefits of Teaching a Baby or Young Child To Read

The following is a list of known benefits of working individually with a baby or young child in teaching them to read. It is important to know that the benefits come from the actual process of working, day in and day out with your child, as well as actually learning how to read. This is not meant to be an exhaustive research article, but a summary of known benefits, many documented in research, and all experienced by parents and teachers.

➤ **Attention – Ability to Focus – Concentration**

➤ **Develops Pattern For Eye Movement** in reading (the lack of this training can result in improper eye tracking, resulting in the interference with reading comprehension)

➤ **Intelligence – Brain Activity – Future Learning Increases**

    a. Vocabulary larger/more sophisticated
    b. Curiosity to ask/learn
    c. Comprehension Skills

➤ **Articulation/Better Speech**

➤ **Hearing/Phonemic Awareness**

➤ **Builds Confidence – Self Esteem**

    a. Makes school easier/more enjoyable
    b. Social interaction more comfortable
    c. More likely to be successful

➤ **Trains Child to Study**

    a. Builds responsibility
    b. Develops perseverance

➤ **Respect for Parent as Teacher and Authority**

    a. Deepens love/bond with parent/child
    b. Improves behavior

➤ **If a Child Has a Learning Disability**, he often ends up several years behind his peers. Starting early can minimize this dilemma.

Here's The Plan:
As Easy as 1, 2, 3

Step 1 **Learning Letter Sounds**
Teach the ABC sounds so that the child knows the sound that each letter makes.

Step 2 **Blending Sounds into Words**
Show that these sounds can be blended together to make words.

Step 3 **Reading Lessons**
Follow the instructions for each lesson. Each lesson will introduce one or more letter combinations or letter sounds. These are called phonics word patterns. Each word pattern will be covered in the 100 lessons. Work with one word pattern until a child can easily read the words in the lists and the sentences.

Optional Activities: Use these recommended techniques to teach Vocabulary Building, Reading Comprehension, Writing Development, and Spelling as the student learns to read beginning on page 247.

Before You Start

➤ In order to work on one skill at a time, you must use a very limited and controlled vocabulary. By careful design, the sentences are written with this in mind. Therefore, in the beginning lessons the sentences must be very simple. The sentences will get more interesting after we learn more words.

➤ The sentences in these lessons are taken from everyday, common language. Your student does not need to understand every word in a sentence in order to learn to read. However, in order to have good reading comprehension, she should understand the meaning of the words. As you cover new words, explain the words to your child. You will have to decide what is necessary for your student to understand. Trust your judgment, and explain as much as you feel is helpful.

➤ As your student masters each lesson, he can read more and more! By the end of lesson 100, your student is reading fluently and has mastered all basic phonics skills.

➤ At the back of this book are flash cards. Photocopy them onto colorful cardstock paper, then cut them up. You may wish to laminate them. You may download them from our website.

➤ Photocopy the Success Chart if you want extra copies for additional students. Choose each student's favorite color.

Letter Sounds and Names

When we use ' ' (single quotation marks) around letters, we are referring to the name of the letter. When we use parentheses ( ), we are referring to the sound they make.

Your student may notice that sometimes the name of a letter is very different than its sound. For example, the letter 'c' is pronounced (c) like the word "cat". The letters 'g', 'h', 'w' and 'y' are also pronounced much differently than their respective names. If your student asks why these letters sound different from their names, explain that we don't know why. It's just one of the many strange things we will be learning which makes learning to read English challenging and fun.

If your student already knows some words that have different sounds for letters, he may get confused. For example, he may ask why the word "like" has a different sound for the 'i' than you are telling him. Or why does the 'c' in the word "cat" sound different than the 'c' in the word "cent"? Explain that we are going to learn the easy words first. Later, we will learn the tricky words.

These tricks and changes will make for an interesting journey as you go through the lessons and learn to read English. Choose to develop a fun attitude towards this journey. Let each new lesson about a "trick" become a major discovery that you get excited about. Enjoy the whole experience with your student and this will be a positive and fun time in your lives together.

Remember, if you have any questions about how a letter or word is pronounced, ask someone who reads and speaks English very well, you can also let Vera Clark show you on the DVD, which will be available soon by ordering online at www.ReadySetReadnow.com.

Important Explanations

➤ It would be wise for you to read every page leading up to Lesson 1 before you start with your child or student. Doing this will help your student succeed. There is more helpful information at the back of the book. Look at the Table of Contents to see what is there.

➤ I use the words "he" and "she" at different times because I don't want to leave boys or girls out.

➤ Throughout this book I may refer to "child" or "student." This in no way means that this book is not for adults who want to learn to read. Some instructions are especially targeted for younger readers, but all lessons apply to someone wanting to learn to read. All of the steps in **As Easy as 1, 2, 3** and many of the other suggestions will fit any new reader. Simply ignore any that do not fit your particular situation.

➤ Notice that we use a traditional, printed "ɑ" and "ɡ" in lessons 1-15. We don't want to confuse the student. The flash cards and sound list use this little "ɑ" and "ɡ" which are the ones we learn to print. After lesson 15, we will transition the student to the type of little "a" and "g" that is used by computers and published materials.

➤ Notice that in the earlier lessons, the size of print is larger than in the later lessons. This is by design. I want the letters to be very easy to see for a young child who is learning to read. Later, when reading becomes easier for the student, we transition to a smaller, more traditional print size.

➤ Explanations of punctuation marks and grammar rules are simplified. For complete information check with a good dictionary or grammar book.

➤ At the beginning of each set of instructions, there MAY be an asterisk (*). That is meant to alert you to something new to teach the student. Explain the new concept to the student, if helpful, and look for how it is used in the vocabulary words, Sight Words or sentences. This is where we teach punctuation and grammar, gradually, as it is needed for our sentences.

➤ DO NOT PROGRESS TO THE NEXT LESSON until the current lesson is mastered. That means it must be fairly easy for the student to read. If you move forward too soon, the student will experience difficulty and frustration. The student will not be successful if pushed too fast.

➤ In the English language, there are words that can have more than one spelling. I had to choose one spelling in order to use the words in a sentence. Therefore, don't worry if you think that the word is spelled differently. It probably is, but it's not the only way. I tried to choose the most commonly used spelling. For example, with the words tepee and teepee (a Native American triangular tent), I chose to use the first spelling, as it is a more traditional spelling of the word in American English.

➤ The instructions for the lessons suggest using a "paper guide." This is simply a piece of blank paper, folded, to make a straight edge to go under the line of words being read. The purpose of a paper guide is to block out distractions and help the student focus on the line being read. You can also use the back side of a bookmark, if it is blank. It is also helpful to use a finger.

➤ For Lessons 1-10, each lesson has its own set of instructions. **Starting with Lesson 11, there is one set of instructions for all of the rest of the lessons (on page 65).** Refer back to page 65 for Lessons 11-100 every time you start a new lesson. Put a bookmark or paperclip there to make it easy to find.

➤ Schools generally teach all phonics skills by the end of third grade. The level of difficulty continues to increase in vocabulary words and content in text books. It is generally understood in the education field that children **learn to read** in grades K-3, and from grades 4 on, they **read to learn**. Therefore, if children are reading by the time they go to kindergarten, they will have a 3-4 year advantage in learning.

➤ With this reading program, a person can learn to read at his own pace. A small child may take 4 years, like in school, whereas an older child or adult may completely learn how to read in a few weeks or months. There are 100 simple lessons. How quickly one progresses depends on his desire, motivation, ability and time available to spend working on it.

Teaching Your Baby

➤ Learn the sounds of the letters. With a baby, show the ABC sound/flash cards while repeating the letter and sound. Continue to do this several times a day. Let your face show that you are happy and excited. Eventually the young child will start to say the letters and sounds with you. If you feel like the child is not paying attention to you, then hold the ABC flash card in front of his face and move it to get his eyes to follow. Move around, maybe his eyes will follow you if you get excited and use a different voice, such as a silly voice.

➤ Read a story to your baby every day, if possible, from a story book. Show colorful pictures to your baby and talk about them.

➤ If a child cannot talk yet, he will still learn the words and sounds. He just can't prove it by telling you. The child may be able to pick the card out that you are talking about. You could even put a few of the cards on the floor and repeat the name and sound of a particular one. Have the child find it for you and bring it to you.

➤ This method of teaching sounds can be used with a person of any age. I have taught the cards with sounds and names to an 11 month old (early talker) and I have taught adults to read.

Baby Talk

➤ I strongly discourage the use of "baby talk" where someone uses improper language to speak to a baby. Children learn to speak what they hear. If we want children to learn to speak correctly, then they need to hear words spoken correctly and clearly. It is difficult for a teacher to correct what a parent has done wrong for years with a child. If a person is used to hearing words spoken incorrectly, it will sound normal and right to him. Remember, we are supposed to model proper behavior as well as speech patterns.

Step 1: Learning Letter Sounds

In Step 1 the student learns and memorizes the basic sound that each letter makes. Some letters can make different sounds at different times. To help a student learn to read we must take one step at a time. In step 3 we will learn the alternative sounds that some letters make at different times.

The Process

Motivation/Excitement

Get excited. Your excitement can be contagious. The first time you sit down to learn the letter sounds with your child, look your child in the eyes and say something like, **"I love you, and I am excited because I am going to teach you how to read!" "Reading is fun!" "You are going to love reading." "You will feel so smart." "After you learn how to read, you will be able to read and learn anything that you want to."** On later occasions you can smile and say **"Let's practice our letters."**

For Babies

Put your baby on your lap and hold him or her to the side so that you can see his or her face. You could also sit across from the baby if the baby can sit up on its own or is in a car seat or other device to support the baby. Just be sure that you are close to your baby. This is quality time that you are spending together. Make sure that your baby is comfortable and alert. Let your face show that you are happy and excited. Then say **"Let's learn our letters so that you can learn to read."**

Introduce Flash Cards

Hold up the flash cards. These can also be called sound cards or ABC cards. If you are working with an older child or an adult then you can say, **"Before we can read, we must learn the code. Words are made up of letters that make sounds. We are going to learn the sounds that these letters make. Let's start!"** An older child or adult will understand what you mean by "code" and it will appeal to his sense of pride to want to figure out the code.

Note: You may choose to use the ABC Sound List or the flash cards at the back of the book.

> **For Babies**
> For young babies, starting around three or four months old, it is best to use the flash cards in the back of the book. You can photocopy them on brightly colored paper and laminate them. Then hold up the stack of flash cards and say **"These are our letters."**

First-Time

The very first time you introduce the letter names and sounds, follow this process. Show the Aa card. Say, **"The name of this letter is 'A'. Here is the big 'A' and here is the little 'a'"** (while you point to the letters). Then say, **"'A' says (a) (a) (turn over) alligator."** Then you stop, point to the alligator and say **"alligator starts with (a) (a). 'A' says (a) (a) alligator."** Go to the next card right away. Show the Bb card and say, **"The name of this letter is 'B'. Here is the big 'B' and here is the little 'b'."** Then say **"'B' says (b) (b) (turn over) bear. Bear starts with (b) (b). 'B' says (b) (b) bear." "The name of this letter is 'C'. Here is the big 'C' and here is the little 'c'. Then say 'C' says (c) (c) (turn over) cat. Cat starts with (c) (c). 'C' says (c) (c) cat. The name of this letter is 'D'. Here is the big 'D' and here is the little 'd'. 'D' says (d) (d) (turn over) 'dog'. Dog starts with (d) (d). 'D' says (d) (d) dog."** Follow this pattern and go through each card. Watch out for the tricky letter 'X'. 'X' says (x) (x) fox. Point out that the 'x' sound is at the end of the word 'fox'.

Practice

On later occasions when you are practicing the letter sounds, you can simplify the process. For example, show the Aa card and say **"A says (a) (a) (turn over quickly) alligator."** Show the Bb card and say **"B says (b) (b) (turn over) bear."** Show the Cc card and say **"C says (c) (c) (turn over) cat."** Show the Dd card and say **"D says (d) (d) (turn over) dog."** It is good for you to go through the flash cards or sound list with your student at least once a day.

If your student is enjoying it and you have the time, you may choose to go through the flash cards or sound list with your student more than once a day. Do not be concerned if you miss one or more days in a row. Remember, the more you can practice with your student the better, but it is not a huge setback if you miss days here or there. Please pay attention to your student. If he or she wants to practice the letters with you, then try to reward that positive behavior. Smile and take the time to sit and practice letters with your student. This is time well spent.

Once your child is familiar with the ABC cards and knows the sounds, it is time to teach him how to put the sounds together to make a word. Move on to Step 2: Blending Sounds into Words.

*See this lesson modeled by Vera Clark on DVD available soon online at www.ReadySetReadnow.com.

For Babies

The first few times you introduce the letter names and sounds to your baby, you should follow the longer script outlined above **"The name of this letter is 'A', here is the big 'A' and here is the little 'a'. The 'A' says (a) (a) like the beginning of 'alligator'."**

If your baby is very young, you may only be able to get through the first five or so letters before he or she is no longer paying attention. This is normal. Put the flash cards away for now and practice again later that day or the following day, starting again from the beginning with the Aa card.

By practicing these flash cards each day, your baby will develop his or her ability to focus. This is a three step process for your baby. First, the baby will listen to you and will begin to memorize the letter sounds. Second, your baby can copy you.

You will be able to tell that your baby is learning the sounds of the letters. He or she may repeat the sounds after you.

Older Babies/Young Children

When you feel your child is ready, you can ask him to repeat the sounds after you. For example, you can say **"'A' says (a) (a) alligator. Can you say (a) (a)?"** Then pause and look at him. Wait for a response and give a positive reaction to your child's effort even if the sound is not perfect. For example, you can say **"Good job, you said (a) (a)!"** You are encouraging your child and reinforcing the correct letter sound. Remember, your child is learning the letter sounds and learning how to pronounce them.

Finally, your baby/child can fill in the blank. When you feel that your child has memorized the letter sounds and can pronounce all or most of the letters, then you can ask him to fill in the blank. For example, you can prompt him, **"What does the letter 'A' say?"** Your child may say (a) (a). If he does not respond then smile and say **"(a) (a) alligator."** This is not a high pressure exercise, but a fun time of learning. When your child fills in all or most of the blanks by telling you the sound of the letters without you having to say the letter sound first, then he is ready to move to Step 2: Blending Sounds in Words.

ABC Sound List

A	**says**	**A**	**a**	**alligator**	
B	**says**	**B**	**b**	**bear**	
C	**says**	**C**	**c**	**cat**	
D	**says**	**D**	**d**	**dog**	
E	**says**	**E**	**e**	**elephant**	
F	**says**	**F**	**f**	**frog**	
G	**says**	**G**	**g**	**gorilla**	
H	**says**	**H**	**h**	**horse**	

I	says	**I**	**i**	iguana	
J	says	**J**	**j**	jaguar	
K	says	**K**	**k**	kangaroo	
L	says	**L**	**l**	lion	
M	says	**M**	**m**	monkey	
N	says	**N**	**n**	nest	
O	says	**O**	**o**	ostrich	
P	says	**P**	**p**	penguin	
Q	says	**Q**	**q**	quail	

R	**says**	**R**	**r**	**rhinoceros**	
S	**says**	**S**	**s**	**seal**	
T	**says**	**T**	**t**	**tiger**	
U	**says**	**U**	**u**	**umbrella**	
V	**says**	**V**	**v**	**vulture**	
W	**says**	**W**	**w**	**whale**	
X	**says**	**X**	**x**	**fox**	
Y	**says**	**Y**	**y**	**yoyo**	
Z	**says**	**Z**	**z**	**zebra**	

Step 2: Blending Sounds into Words

Once your student has mastered the basic sounds of the letters, we are ready to learn how to put the sounds together to make a word. This can be called blending sounds.

Here are the instructions that go with the lesson on the next few pages. As you will see, we will be working with letters. It is best if you write the letters out yourself, while talking with your student. **However, if you prefer, you can use the letters which are written out for you on the next two pages.** You should use a white board with markers, or paper and a thick marker. A pencil or pen will work, but they are not as interesting to look at as a thick marker. The younger the child, the larger and more colorful you should make the letters to hold his attention.

Instructions

1. Start by drawing the letter 'c'. Say, **"What *sound* does this letter make?"** The response should be (c) as in "c̲at," since you have already taught your student the sound cards. Say, **"Good!"** If he says the name of the letter 'c', then say, **"The *name* of this letter is 'c', but the *sound* is (c)."**

2. Now draw the letter 'a'. Say, **"What *sound* does this letter make?"** The response should be (a) as in "ca̲t." Say, **"That's right!"**

3. Now draw the letters 'c' and 'a' together. Say, **"Now let's put these sounds together."** Then you put your hand under the 'c' as you make the (c) sound, and drag your hand to the right under the 'a' as you make the (a) sound. Then sound out **"c...a...."**

4. Now draw the letter 't' after the 'ca' and say, **"Let's put these sounds together."** Drag your hand to the right under all three letters and say **"cat."** I intentionally don't have a child sound out the last letter by itself because if it is the last thing the student hears or thinks about, sometimes they will start the word with that sound.

5. If your student is young, this should generate some excited talk about kitty cats. If your student is reading for the first time, this is a moment where a breakthrough starts to happen.

6. Then say, **"That is how we read!"** **"We are learning the secret code, and finding out how easy and fun it is to read!"**

7. Now you get to play with the word "cat." Erase the 'c' and replace it with any of the following letters: 'f', 'b', 'h', 'p', 'r', 'm', and 's', showing the student how we make new words by changing one letter.

8. Now you can play with the word "cat", by changing the last letter 't', and replacing it with 'p' or 'n'.

9. Now we are ready to start lesson 1! You can do this! Get excited and tell the student things like this: **"We are ready to start with lesson 1!" "Now we will learn to read more words." "This will be fun." "You are going to be even smarter because you are learning to read!"**

For Babies

If you are working with a baby or toddler, it is possible that he may be comfortable at Step 2 and may not want to move on to reading sentences in Step 3 until he has attained more maturity. If that is the case with your student, continue to practice Step 2 Blending Sounds into Words and continue reading to your child, pointing to the words as you read.

---

*See this lesson modeled by Vera Clark on DVD available soon online at www.ReadySetReadnow.com.

Blending Lesson

Say the sounds of the letters below. We start with the word "cat," then change the first letter to make new words. Start at the left; then move to the right, sounding out what you see.

c . . . . . a . . . . . ca . . . . cat

r . . . . . a . . . . . ra . . . . rat

b . . . . . a . . . . ba . . . bat

s . . . . . a . . . . . sa . . . . sat

f . . . . . a . . . . . . fa . . . . . fat

h . . . . . a . . . . . . ha . . . hat

m . . . . . a . . . . . . ma . . . mat

p . . . . . a . . . . . pa . . . pat

Now we are starting with "can" and changing the first letter to make new words.

c . . . . . a . . . . ca . . . . can

b . . . . . a . . . . ba . . . ban

f . . . . . a . . . . . fa . . . . fan

m . . . . . a . . . . . ma . . . man

N . . . . . a . . . . . Na . . . Nan

p . . . . . a . . . . . pa . . . pan

r . . . . . a . . . . . ra . . . ran

t . . . . . a . . . . . ta . . . tan

v . . . . . a . . . . . va . . . van

Step 3: Reading Lessons

Lesson Index

Here is an index showing which phonics skill is being addressed in each lesson.

1.	__an	26.	sc sk sm sn sp st sw tw__
2.	__at	27.	Multiple Cons. Blends
3.	__ad	28.	__ang ing ong ung
4.	__ag	29.	__ank ink onk unk
5.	__ap	30.	Contractions n't
6.	__am	31.	Contractions 'd, 'll, 've, 's, 're, 'm
7.	__ab	32.	sh
8.	__ax __al	33.	th
9.	__it	34.	ch
10.	__in	35.	tch
11.	__ig	36.	wh qu
12.	__id	37.	ee
13.	__im __ip	38.	ea
14.	_en _on _un	39.	oo
15.	_eg _og _ug	40.	oo
16.	_et _ot _ut	41.	Suffix ed
17.	_d _p	42.	Suffix es s
18.	_b _x _s _m	43.	Suffix er
19.	_ss nn ll gg ff zz dd	44.	Ending er
20.	_ck	45.	Suffix er est ness
21.	_st _sk	46.	Suffix y ly ily
22.	_nd _nt	47.	y ies ied
23.	_mp ft lt lf lp ld pt xt lk ct	48.	en ie ies ied
24.	br cr dr fr gr pr tr__	49.	__le
25.	bl cl fl gl pl sl__	50.	_el _al

➤ We use a blank line before or after a letter or combination of letters to show that it is a beginning or ending sound of a word. Other letters would traditionally fill in the blank; for example, Lesson 1 teaches the __an words, such as *can, fan,* and *man.*

51. _in _on _ain	76. Sound of (or) oor our ar oar
52. _et _it _ic _ish	77. Sound of (air) ear eir arr ar
53. _ful	78. Sound of (e) ea ai ie u ue
54. ai	79. Sound of (oo) u o
55. ay	80. Sound of (oo) ue ew ui oe o_e
56. oa	81. Sound of (ee) ine ile ey ie ei Sound of (i) u ui ine
57. Sound of long o ow	82. Sound of (u) o ou oo o_e
58. ou	83. Long a
59. ow	84. Long e
60. aw au	85. Long i
61. oi oy	86. Long o
62. _a _ent	87. Sound of long u u ou
63. a_ be_	88. Soft c
64. e_ de_	89. Soft g
65. re_ pre_ in_	90. dge gh ch
66. Silent e (a_e)	91. ph, unusual s
67. Silent e (i_e)	92. igh aigh eigh ough augh
68. Silent e (o_e)	93. Silent Letters l b
69. Silent e (u_e) & (e_e)	94. Silent Letters k t
70. or	95. Silent Letter w
71. ar	96. Silent Letter h d c p s n
72. er	97. _tion sion cian
73. ir	98. _ture
74. ur	99. _tious cious ous eous
75. Sound of (er) or ar	100. _tial cial tient cient tual

➤ We use a blank line before or after a letter or combination of letters to show that it is a beginning or ending sound of a word. Other letters would traditionally fill in the blank; for example, Lesson 1 teaches the _an words, such as *can, fan,* and *man.*

➤ We use parenthesis around a letter or letter combination to refer to the sound that it makes.

Success Chart

Instructions Use the Success Chart by writing in the date and checking off each lesson when your student can read the entire lesson well without sounding out any words. The lesson includes every part of the lesson: the <u>Vocabulary Words</u>, the <u>Sight Words</u>, AND all of the <u>Sentences</u>. This Chart will be a journal with dates that you can review to remember when your student learned to read and at what pace. Celebrate every time a lesson is checked off and dated. It doesn't have to be a big celebration, but you need to keep the fun in it and keep the student motivated to keep on going!

In order for your student to learn to read successfully, you MUST **<u>NOT</u>** GO ON TO THE NEXT LESSON, unless the current lesson has been learned well and is easy for the student to read. That means, you stay on the SAME lesson and repeat it for as many days as it takes for the student to learn it well. It is good to go back to previous lessons for review. If your student is feeling discouraged and says "I can't read!" then respond, **"You really can read, and I can show you!"** You then go back to an earlier, easier lesson that the student has already mastered, and have her read it. You then say, **"You are reading this lesson, which means you can read! You will be able to read another lesson after we practice it enough."** Then say other words of encouragement to help the student not give up. Here are some examples:

"We are strong, and we don't give up." "Not everything is easy, but we work hard and it is worth it." You might want to reward the student for good effort and praise him for trying. Don't make the reading session too long. Try to keep it short and happy. For a young child, 10 or 15 minutes might be too long. Do what is best for your student, and remember, too short is better than too long. We don't want our children to hate reading.

Keep in mind that you want to build up your child's self-esteem. We want to learn, but in a positive way. Always be kind and gentle with your student. Be firm only if necessary.

Let's talk more about how to celebrate your student completing a lesson. The way you celebrate depends on whether the lesson was easy or hard to master. Was the lesson completed in a short time or a long time? If it was completed within a short time, then it may be enough to show pride with a big smile, a high-five, and words of encouragement. If it took a long time, then make a bigger deal about it. You may dance around the room and squeal with laughter! Maybe a little prize is in order. It is your decision on an appropriate way to reward a student. You know the child and his personality best. When my daughter, Katie, was learning to read, I took her to the doughnut store when she reached certain reading milestones. When she was 3 years old, she was reading at a first grade level. When my son, Eric, was learning to read, he became bored with daily practicing. He was four years old and was reading at a first grade level. I knew he was motivated by money, so I paid him a nickel for each page he read. Then he eagerly read his pages and was reading at a second grade level when he went to kindergarten at age five. But just a word of caution: we don't want to overdo our celebration or spend too much money and spoil the child. Remember, there are 100 lessons and we don't want the student to expect a big reward each time.

Success Chart

Student Name_____

Step 1._____

Step 2 _____

Step 3

1.	26.	51.	76.
2.	27.	52.	77.
3.	28.	53.	78.
4.	29.	54.	79.
5.	30.	55.	80.
6.	31.	56.	81.
7.	32.	57.	82.
8.	33.	58.	83.
9.	34.	59.	84.
10.	35.	60.	85.
11.	36.	61.	86.
12.	37.	62.	87.
13.	38.	63.	88.
14.	39.	64.	89.
15.	40.	65.	90.
16.	41.	66.	91.
17.	42.	67.	92.
18.	43.	68.	93.
19.	44.	69.	94.
20.	45.	70.	95.
21.	46.	71.	96.
22.	47.	72.	97.
23.	48.	73.	98.
24.	49.	74.	99.
25.	50.	75.	100.

*Check off and date after each step or lesson is mastered.

Are you ready?
Let's have fun!

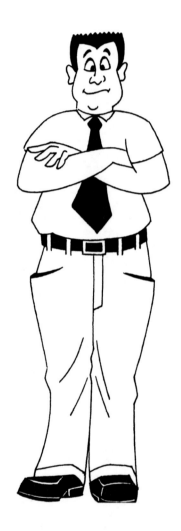

Instructions: Lesson 1

1. Practice saying the ABC sound list or flash cards.

2. Talk with your student about the pattern of words. Explain that **"The words all end with 'an'. They have a different beginning letter and sound. These words rhyme, because they sound the same except for a different beginning sound."**

3. Show your student the words that start with a capital letter and say, **"This is a capital letter. We also call capital letters upper case and big letters. Words start with a capital letter if it is a name, the first word in a sentence, or the word 'I.'"**

4. Practice reading the **Vocabulary Words**. Tell your student what each word says and ask her to repeat after you. These words can be sounded out because the letters have the same sound as in the ABC sound list and flash cards. Show her how to sound it out. The best way is to say (c), (a), (ca), "can" while you run your finger or pencil under the word "can".

5. Have your student repeat the **Sight Words** after you, and say, **"We must memorize these words instead of sounding them out because some don't have the sounds we have learned. That means some are tricky."**

6. After reading Sentence #1, explain that a sentence is a complete thought that is said or written. Explain that **"A period (.) is at the end of a sentence that makes a statement."** Example: "I ran to the van."

7. Before reading Sentence #6, explain that **"An exclamation point (!) is at the end of a sentence that tells something exciting or tells something in a strong or forceful way."** Example: "Don't run into the street!"

8. Before reading Sentence #7, explain that **"A question mark (?) is at the end of a sentence that asks a question."** Example: "What is your name?"

9. Have your student read each word and all of the sentences while using a paper guide, bookmark, or finger to help your student not get distracted or lost.

10. Ask student to find the sentence that goes with the drawing. (See Answer Key, page 261)

11. Have your student read each of the sentences again.

12. Keep practicing this lesson until the words and sentences can be read easily and correctly. DO NOT go on to the next lesson until then.

13. Encourage your student by saying things like: **"You are working hard!" "I am proud of you!" "You are a good reader!" "You are smart!"**

14. Date and check off on Student's Success Chart when this lesson has been completed.

*Optional Activities: Refer to the Table of Contents for Vocabulary Building, Reading Comprehension, Writing Development, and **Spelling**. NOTE: Do not start doing the writing and spelling activities if the student is too young or protests strongly. He may stop reading altogether. However, it is logical to learn to spell and write what can be read. Age 4 is a good time to start teaching writing and spelling.

Lesson 1   __an

Vocabulary Words			Sight Words
ban	pan	Dan	I
can	ran	Jan	the
fan	tan	Nan	to
man	van		is

Sentences

1. I ran to the van.

2. Nan ran to Dan.

3. The man can fan.

4. I can fan Nan.

5. The man is Dan.

6. Dan ran to the tan van!

7. Is the pan tan?

8. The pan is tan.

9. Is the van tan?

10. The van is tan.

11. Is the man tan?

12. The man is tan.

13. Can I fan Jan?

14. I can fan Jan.

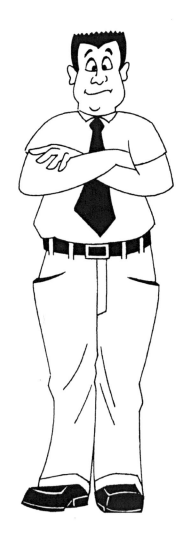

Find the sentence in the lesson!

Instructions: Lesson 2

1. Practice saying the ABC sound list or flash cards.

2. Talk with your student about the pattern of words. Explain that **"The words all end with 'at'. They have a different beginning letter and sound. These words rhyme, because they sound the same except for a different beginning sound."**

3. **"These words can be sounded out because the letters have the same sound as in the ABC sound list and flash cards."** Show him how to sound it out. The best way is to say (c), (a), (ca), "cat" while you run your finger or pencil under the word "cat."

4. Practice reading the Vocabulary Words. Tell your student what each word says and ask him to repeat after you

5. Have your student repeat the Sight Words after you and say, **"We must memorize these words because they won't always have the sounds we have learned from the ABC sound list."**

6. Explain that one word can be used in different ways. For example, in sentence #4, the word "pat" means to tap lightly with fingers. In sentence #6, "Pat" is used as a person's name.

7. Have your student read each word and all of the sentences while using a paper guide or bookmark to help your student not get distracted or lost.

8. Did you find the sentence that goes with the drawing?   (See Answer Key, page 261)

9. Have your student read each of the sentences again.

10. Keep practicing this lesson until the words and sentences can be read easily and correctly. DO NOT go on to the next lesson until then.

11. Encourage your student by saying things like: **"You are working hard!" "I am proud of you!" "You are a good reader!" "You are smart!"**

12. Date and check off on Student's Success Chart when this lesson has been completed.

    *Optional Activities: Refer to the Table of Contents for Vocabulary Building, Reading Comprehension, Writing Development, and Spelling.

Lesson 2 ___at

Vocabulary Words			Sight Words
at	cat	hat	a
bat	fat	mat	and
pat	sat	rat	are
vat			on

Sentences

1. The cat is fat.

2. A rat ran to the mat.

3. The rat and I sat.

4. Can Dan pat the bat?

5. Dan can pat the bat.

6. Is Pat at the van?

7. Pat is at the van.

8. Are the cat and rat fat?

9. The cat and rat are fat.

10. A fat cat sat on the hat.

11. The rat sat on the bat.

12. Is Nan on the mat?

13. Nan sat on the mat.

14. Is the rat on the bat?

15. The rat is on the bat.

Find the sentence in the lesson!

Instructions: Lesson 3

1. Practice saying the ABC sound list or flash cards.

2. Talk with your student about the pattern of words. Explain that **"The words all end with 'ad' but have a different beginning letter and sound, which means they rhyme."**

3. Show your student how to sound out the words. The best way is to say (d), (a), (da), "dad" while you run your finger or pencil under the word "dad".

4. Practice reading the Vocabulary Words. Tell your student what each word says and ask her to repeat after you.

5. Have your student repeat the Sight Words after you and say, **"We must memorize these words because they won't always have the sounds we have learned from the ABC sound list."**

6. Encourage your student to ask the meaning of any word. This can lead to very good discussions that will increase your student's understanding and ability to communicate. This will also help your relationship because you care enough to take time to teach her. It is okay to say, "I'm not sure what that means."

7. Have your student read each word and all of the sentences while using a paper guide or bookmark to help your student not get distracted or lost.

8. Did you find the sentence that goes with the drawing? (See Answer Key, page 261)

9. Have your student read each of the sentences again.

10. Keep practicing this lesson until the words and sentences can be read easily and correctly. DO NOT go on to the next lesson until then.

11. Encourage your student by saying things like: **"You are working hard!" "I am proud of you!" "You are a good reader!" "With each lesson you get better!" "You are smart!"**

12. Date and check off on Student's Success Chart when this lesson has been completed.

    *Optional Activities: Refer to the Table of Contents for Vocabulary Building, Reading Comprehension, Writing Development, and Spelling.

Lesson 3   _ad

Vocabulary Words			Sight Words
bad	fad	rad	has
cad	mad	sad	was
dad	pad	Tad	not

Sentences

1. Dan has a rat.

2. Is the rat bad?

3. The rat is bad!

4. Dad is mad at the rat.

5. The rat is on the pad.

6. Pat had a tan cat.

7. The cat ran to the pad.

8. The cat and rat are mad!

9. Dan has a mad rat.

10. I ran to the pad and sat.

11. Nan and I had the mat.

12. The rat was not bad.

13. Was Dad mad?

14. Dad was not mad and Dan was not sad.

15. I am not mad and I am not sad.

Find the sentence in the lesson!

Instructions: Lesson 4

1. Practice saying the ABC sound list or flash cards.

2. Talk with your student about the pattern of words. Explain that **"The words all end with 'ag' but have a different beginning letter and sound, which means they rhyme."**

3. Show your student how to sound out words. The best way is to say (b), (a), (ba), "bag" while you run your finger or pencil under the word "bag."

4. Practice reading the Vocabulary Words. Tell your student what each word says and ask him to repeat after you.

5. Have your student repeat the Sight Words after you and say, **"We must memorize these words."**

6. Encourage your student to ask the meaning of any word. This can lead to very good discussions that will increase your student's understanding and ability to communicate. This will also help your relationship because you care enough to take time to teach her. It is okay to say, "I'm not sure what that means."

7. Have your student read each word and all of the sentences while using a paper guide or bookmark.

8. Did you find the sentence that goes with the drawing?   (See Answer Key, page 261)

9. Have your student read each of the sentences again.

10. Keep practicing this lesson until the words and sentences can be read easily and correctly. DO NOT go on to the next lesson until then.

11. Encourage your student by saying things like: **"You are working hard!" "I am proud of you!" "You are a good reader!" "With each lesson you get better!" "You are smart!"**

12. Date and check off on Student's Success Chart when this lesson has been completed.

    *Optional Activities: Refer to the Table of Contents for Vocabulary Building, Reading Comprehension, Writing Development, and Spelling.

Lesson 4

_ag

Vocabulary Words			Sight Words
bag	jag	rag	in
gag	lag	sag	into
hag	nag	tag	it
		wag	put

Sentences

1. Has Dad put a rag into the bag?

2. Dad put a rag into the bag.

3. Pat put the bag into a van.

4. Can I tag Dan?

5. I can tag Dan and Nan.

6. Can Dad put the hat in the van?

7. Dad has put the hat into the van.

8. The bag can sag.

9. Can the cat wag in the bag?

10. The cat can wag.

11. Put the fan in the van.

12. I had a bag and Nan put a rag in it.

13. I can pat the cat and it can wag.

14. Can Dad put the cat into the van?

15. Dad can put the cat into the van.

Find the sentence
in the lesson!

Instructions: Lesson 5

1. Practice saying the ABC sound list or flash cards.

2. Talk about the pattern of words. Explain that **"The words all end with 'ap' but have a different beginning letter and sound. They rhyme."**

3. Show your student how to sound out the words. The best way is to say (l), (a), (la), "lap" while you run your finger or pencil under the word "lap."

4. Practice reading the Vocabulary Words. Tell your student what each word says and ask her to repeat after you.

5. Have your student repeat the Sight Words and memorize them.

6. Sentence #12 uses the words "can not". More often this is spelled as one word "cannot," but it is also spelled in two words. In order to make it easier to read, we will continue to use the two-word spelling "can not."

7. Explain that **"There is an ('s) at the end of a word which shows that something belongs to it (a possession). That little mark is called an "apostrophe."** Example: "Sam's dog" means the dog belongs to Sam."

8. Explain that **"An 's' goes at the end of a word when it means more than one (plural)."** Example: "one dog" or "two dogs."

9. Encourage your student to ask the meaning of any word. This can lead to very good discussions that will increase your student's understanding and ability to communicate. This will also help your relationship because you care enough to take time to teach her. It is okay to say, "I'm not sure what that means."

10. If a word is difficult to explain, or it is beyond a student's understanding, it is fine to say, "This is just a silly word" or "This word just makes a noise." Example: "tap"

11. Have your student read each word and all of the sentences while using a paper guide.

12. Did you find the sentence that goes with the drawing? (See Answer Key, page 261)

13. Have your student read each of the sentences again.

14. Keep practicing this lesson until the words and sentences can be read easily and correctly. DO NOT go on to the next lesson until then.

15. Encourage your student by saying things like: **"You are working hard!" "I am proud of you!" "You are a good reader!" "With each lesson you get better!" "You are smart!"**

16. Date and check off on Student's Success Chart when this lesson has been completed.

    *Optional Activities: Refer to the Table of Contents for Vocabulary Building, Reading Comprehension, Writing Development, and Spelling.

Lesson 5 __ap

Vocabulary Words			Sight Words
cap	map	sap	her
gap	nap	tap	his
lap	rap	yap	have

Sentences

1. Is Pat's cap on her lap?

2. Pat's cap is on her lap.

3. Can Dad put a map in his bag?

4. Dad can put maps into his bag.

5. Can Dan have a nap in his van?

6. Dan can have a nap in his van.

7. Can I tap and rap on the van?

8. I can tap and rap on the van.

9. Can Nan yap and yap?

10. Dan is mad. His van has sap on it.

11. Can Dan have a nap in Dad's van?

12. Dan can not have his nap in
Dad's van.

13. Dan and Dad have maps and caps.

14. Pat can not yap in the van.

15. Dad has Jan on his lap.

Find the sentence in the lesson!

Instructions: Lesson 6

1. Practice saying the ABC sound list or flash cards.

2. Talk about the pattern of words. Explain that **"The words all end with 'am'."**

3. Show your student how to sound out the words. The best way is to say (j), (a), (ja), "jam".

4. Practice reading the Vocabulary Words. Tell your student what each word says and ask him to repeat after you.

5. Have your student repeat the Sight Words and memorize them.

6. Pointing to a comma, explain that **"(,) is a comma, and it can mean to wait a tiny bit."** In lessons 10, 11, and 16 we will learn additional ways to use the comma.

7. Encourage your student to ask the meaning of any word. This can lead to very good discussions that will increase student's understanding and ability to communicate. This will also help your relationship because you care enough to take time to teach her.

8. If a word is difficult to explain, or it is beyond a student's understanding, it is fine to say **"We will learn about this word later."** In sentence 14, you'll read the word "bam". You can explain to your student that "The word 'bam' describes a noise."

9. Optional: Explain that an exclamation point (!) can be used at the end of a sentence and also inside a sentence. For example, in sentence #14, "Nan went bam! bam! on Sam's van." (see Lesson 1 instructions for more information on use of exclamation point).

10. Remind your student that one word can be used in different ways. For example, in Sentence #4, "Pam <u>can</u> have the jam in the <u>can</u>," the word "can" is used two times. The first time "can" means "is able to"; the second time "can" means a container.

11. Have your student read each word and all of the sentences while using a paper guide.

12. Did you find the sentence that goes with the drawing? (See Answer Key, page 261)

13. Have your student read each of the sentences again.

14. Keep practicing this lesson until the words and sentences can be read easily and correctly. DO NOT go on to the next lesson until then.

15. Encourage your student by saying things like: **"You are working hard!" "I am proud of you!" "You are a good reader!" "You are smart!"**

16. Date and check off on Student's Success Chart when this lesson has been completed.

    *Optional Activities: Refer to the Table of Contents for Vocabulary Building, Reading Comprehension, Writing Development, and Spelling.

Lesson 6 _am

Vocabulary Words			Sight Words
am	yam	Sam	get
bam	ram	Pam	go
jam	ham	Tam	went
			will

Sentences

1. Am I Sam?

2. I am Sam.

3. Can Pam have the jam?

4. Pam can have the jam in the can.

5. Can Dad get the ham?

6. Dad can go get the ham in the tan can.

7. Can Dan ram the van?

8. Dan can not ram the van!

9. Pam will get the yams.

10. Go get the yams, Pam!

11. Put the yams into the can, Nan!

12. Tam will put the ham into a can.

13. Tam and Jan went to get the can.

14. Nan went bam! bam! on Sam's van.

15. Sam was mad at Nan!

Find the sentence in the lesson!

Instructions: Lesson 7

1. Practice saying the ABC sound list or flash cards.

2. Talk about the pattern of words. Explain that **"The words all end with 'ab'."**

3. Show your student how to sound out the words.

4. Practice reading the Vocabulary Words. Tell your student what each word says and ask her to repeat after you, or have him read them first if he chooses.

5. Have your student repeat and memorize the Sight Words.

6. Encourage your student to ask the meaning of any word. For example, explain that "lab" is short for "labrador", or "laboratory"; "jab" means to poke; "gab" means to talk a lot; "dab" means to touch something, as with a cloth; "nab" means to take; and "cab" is short for taxi cab or the cabin of a truck. This can lead to very good discussions that will increase your student's understanding and ability to communicate.

5. If a word is difficult to explain, or it is beyond a student's understanding, it is fine to say **"We will learn about this word later."** You can also look up the definition of a word in the dictionary.

6. Have your student read each word and all of the sentences using a paper guide.

7. Did you find the sentence that goes with the drawing? (See Answer Key, page 261)

8. Have your student read each of the sentences again.

9. Reminder: It is good to go back and have student read previous lessons.

10. Keep practicing this lesson until the words and sentences can be read easily and correctly. DO NOT go on to the next lesson until then.

11. Encourage your student by saying things like: **"You are working hard!" "I am proud of you!" "You are a good reader!" "You get better each time!" You are smart!"**

12. Date and check off on Student's Success Chart when this lesson has been completed.

   *Optional Activities: Refer to the Table of Contents for Vocabulary Building, Reading Comprehension, Writing Development, and Spelling.

Lesson 7 ___ab

Vocabulary Words			Sight Words
cab	jab	Tab	does
dab	lab		our
gab	nab		name
			we

Sentences

1. Jan and I have a tan lab.

2. Does our lab have a name?

3. Our lab does have a name, Tab.

4. Will Tab nab Dad's hat?

5. Tab will not nab Dad's hat.

6. Tab can wag and wag.

7. Can we get in a cab?

8. We can get in the cab and gab.

9. I can jab Nan and Pat.

10. We can jab and tag and gab.

11. Can Pam get the rag and dab it?

12. Get the rag and dab it, Pam!

13. Can Pat get her bag and put it in the cab?

14. Pat will get her bag and put it in the cab.

15. Pat, go get the bag to put in the cab!

Find the sentence in the lesson!

Instructions: Lesson 8

1. Practice saying the ABC sound list or flash cards.

2. Talk about the pattern of words. Explain that **"The words all end with 'ax' or 'al'.**

3. Show your student how to sound out the words.

4. Practice reading the Vocabulary Words. Tell your student what each word says and ask him to repeat after you, or have him read them first if he chooses.

5. Have your student repeat and memorize the Sight Words.

6. Explain that the word "an" means the same as the word "a" but it is only used before a word that begins with a vowel such as 'a', 'e', 'i', 'o', 'u' or a vowel sound such as silent 'h' as in "hour" or "honest". Example: <u>an</u> egg, <u>an</u> umbrella, <u>an</u> apple, <u>an</u> hour, *or* <u>a</u> cat, <u>a</u> bear.

7. Encourage your student to ask the meaning of any word. For example, explain that "sax" is short for "saxophone"; a "lad" is a boy; "lax" can mean relaxed.

8. If a word is difficult to explain, or it is beyond a student's understanding, it is fine to say **"We will learn about this word later,"** or **"I'm not sure what it means."** You can also look up the definition of a word in the dictionary.

9. Have your student read each word and all of the sentences while using a paper guide.

10. Did you find the sentence that goes with the drawing? (See Answer Key, page 261)

11. Have your student read each of the sentences again.

12. Keep practicing this lesson until the words and sentences can be read easily and correctly. DO NOT go on to the next lesson until then.

13. Optional: Occasionally have your student read previous lessons to encourage her with how well she is reading.

14. Date and check off on Student's Success Chart when this lesson has been completed.

15. Encourage your student by saying things like: **"You are working hard!" "I am proud of you!" "You are a good reader!" "You are smart!"**

   *Optional Activities: Refer to the Table of Contents for Vocabulary Building, Reading Comprehension, Writing Development, and Spelling.

Lesson 8

__ax __al

Vocabulary Words			Sight Words
ax	wax	pal	an
lax	tax	Al	of
sax	Max	Hal	play
		Sal	with

Sentences

1. The man has a lad with the name, Al.

2. The man is lax with Al and his pal.

3. Al's pal is Hal, and Sal's pal is Pam.

4. The name of her pal is Sal.

5. Dad and Sam have an ax.

6. Max and Hal play the sax.

7. Max can play his sax.

8. He can put wax on his ax.

9. We can play with the cats in our laps.

10. Al and Hal can not get the ax.

11. Sal and Max can play the sax.

12. Go get the sax, Sal!

13. Dad and Al have a vat of wax.

14. Sal put Max's sax in the vat of wax!

Find the sentence in the lesson!

Instructions: Lesson 9

1. Practice saying the ABC sound list or flash cards.

2. Talk about the pattern of words. Explain that **"We are learning something new. These words all end with 'it'."**

3. Show your student how to sound out the words.

4. Practice reading the Vocabulary Words. Tell your student what each word says and ask him to repeat after you.

5. Have your student repeat and memorize the Sight Words.

6. As we learned in Lesson 6, a comma (,) can tell the reader to pause. In addition, a pair of commas can be used to set apart certain information in a sentence. This is called a comma clause. Example: Sam, a cat, ran to the van. Here the comma clause describes Sam by explaining that he is a cat.

7. Encourage your student to ask the meaning of any word. For example, a "wick" is the part of a candle that is lit on fire; "wit" can mean to be clever; "pit" is a hole.

8. If a word is difficult to explain, or it is beyond a student's understanding, it is fine to say, **"We'll know more when it is used in a sentence,"** or "I'm not sure." You can also look up the definition of a word in the dictionary.

9. Have your student read each word and all of the sentences while using a paper guide.

10. Have your student read each of the sentences again.

11. Did you find the sentence that goes with the drawing? (See Answer Key, page 261)

12. Keep practicing this lesson until the words and sentences can be read easily and correctly. DO NOT go on to the next lesson until then.

13. Optional: Occasionally have your student read previous lessons to encourage her with how well she is reading.

14. Encourage your student by saying things like: **"You are working hard!" "I am proud of you!" "You are a good reader!" "You are smart!"**

15. Date and check off on Student's Success Chart when this lesson has been completed.

*Optional Activities: Refer to the Table of Contents for Vocabulary Building, Reading Comprehension, Writing Development, and Spelling.

Lesson 9   _it

Vocabulary Words			Sight Words
it	hit	pit	got
bit	kit	sit	she
fit	lit	wit	wick

Sentences

1. Sam, the cat, bit a rat and it got mad.

2. Kit, the rat, will fit into the vat.

3. Dan has a kit and Hal hit it.

4. Hal is not Dan's pal.

5. Dan got mad at Hal.

6. Dad lit the wick on the wax.

7. Sal went to sit in the pit.

8. Pam will go sit with Sal.

9. Will Pat gab and gab with Sal?

10. She will gab and gab!

11. Dan will play with Sal.

12. Max sat in the pit with Al and Kit.

13. Sal will have a fit!

14. Dan and his pal, Sal, fit in the pit.

Find the sentence in the lesson!

Instructions: Lesson 10

1. Practice saying the ABC sound list or flash cards.

2. Talk about the pattern of words. Explain that **"The words all end with 'in'."**

3. Show your student how to sound out the words.

4. Practice reading the Vocabulary Words. Tell your student what each word says and ask her to repeat after you.

5. Have your student repeat and memorize the Sight Words.

6. Encourage your student to ask the meaning of any word. For example, explain that "kin" means someone that is related to you. If a word is difficult to explain, or it is beyond a student's understanding, it is fine to say, **"We'll know more when it is used in a sentence,"** or "I don't know." You can also look up the meaning of a word in the dictionary.

7. Have your student read each word and all of the sentences while using a paper guide.

8. Did you find the sentence that goes with the drawing? (See Answer Key, page 261)

9. Have your student read each of the sentences again.

10. Keep practicing this lesson until the words and sentences can be read easily and correctly. DO NOT go on to the next lesson until then.

11. Optional: Occasionally have your student read previous lessons to encourage her with how well she is reading.

12. Encourage your student by saying things like: **"You are working hard!" "I am proud of you!" "You are a good reader!" "You are smart!"**

13. Date and check off on Student's Success Chart when this lesson has been completed.

    *Optional Activities: Refer to the Table of Contents for Vocabulary Building, Reading Comprehension, Writing Development, and Spelling.

Lesson 10 _in

Vocabulary Words			Sight Words
in	fin	sin	do
bin	kin	tin	he
din	pin	win	two
			what
			if

Sentences

1. What does Sal have?

2. Sal has a fin.

3. Max has two fins.

4. Max is Sal's kin.

5. Put the fins into the bin!

6. Can Pam put the pin on the hat?

7. Nan put the ham in the tin can.

8. Will he win the sax?

9. What will he do with the sax if he wins?

10. He will play the sax with his pals.

11. Hal and Max have two pins.

12. Max and Sal are kin to Sam and Dan.

13. What do I do with a fin, put it on?

14. Can Max play with an ax?

15. Max, do not play with an ax!

Find the sentence in the lesson!

Instructions Page for Lessons 11-100

1. Practice saying the ABC flash cards if needed.

2. Present the new sounds introduced in the lesson and talk about the pattern of words.

3. Have your student sound out the new words.

4. Practice reading the Vocabulary Words. Tell your student what each word says and ask him to repeat after you. If your student wants to, he can try them himself first.

5. Have your student repeat and memorize the Sight Words.

6. Encourage your student to ask the meaning of any word. If a word is difficult to explain, or it is beyond a student's understanding, it is fine to say, "We will learn about this word later." You can also look up the definition of a word in the dictionary.

7. If there is an asterisk * under the Vocabulary Word box, then there is something new to learn. You decide if your student needs to know or is ready to learn it. Some are explanations for the teacher.

8. Have your student read each word and all of the sentences while using a paper guide.

9. Did you find the sentence that goes with the drawing? (See Answer Key, page 261)

10. Have your student read each of the sentences again.

11. Keep practicing this lesson until the words and sentences can be read easily and correctly. DO NOT go on to the next lesson until then.

12. Optional: Occasionally have your student read previous lessons to encourage her with how well she is reading.

13. Encourage your student by saying things like: **"You are working hard!" "I am proud of you!" "You are a good reader!" "You are smart!"**

14. Date and check off on Student's Success Chart when this lesson has been completed.

    *Optional Activities: Refer to the Table of Contents for Vocabulary Building, Reading Comprehension, Writing Development, and Spelling.

    Note: Starting with Lesson 11, there is one set of instructions for all of the rest of the lessons. Refer back to this Instructions Page for Lessons 11-100 every time you start a new lesson. Put a paper clip here.

Lesson 11   _ig

Vocabulary Words			Sight Words	
big	gig	rig	by	you
dig	jig	wig	my	want
fig	pig		pay	Mom

✽ Some words change based on the way they are used in the sentence. For example, in sentence #1 Dad "want<u>s</u>" something, but in sentence #2 Mom does not "want" him to get it. As you come across these changes, point out to your student <u>if helpful</u>.

✽ A comma can be used with a conjunction (for, and, nor, but, or, yet, so) to join two simple sentences. For example, see sentence #11.

✽ See Instructions Page 65.

Sentences

1. My dad wants to get a big rig.

2. Mom does not want him to get it.

3. He will pay for the rig and pay the tax.

4. Pam wants to dig a big pit.

5. Pam, will you put the cans by the pit?

6. Dan's cat can do a jig.

7. Can Nan and Pat have a fig?

8. Dan can put a wig on his pig.

9. Dad does not want to have a fig.

10. Will you pay for the wig?

11. Dad's big rig is tan, and he will sit in it.

12. Sal will do a jig by the big pit.

13. Max and Dan are in Dad's big rig.

14. I want to get a big pig and name it Max!

15. The name of his gig is Rap and Jam.

Lesson 12   _id

Vocabulary Words			Sight Words	
bid	kid	rid	yes	day
did	lid	Sid	no	today
hid	mid			when

✴ A hyphen (-) is a short line used to connect parts of words. For example: "mid-day" in sentence 9, means "in the middle of the day."

✴ See Instructions Page 65.

Sentences

1. Did Dad put a bid on the van?

2. Yes, Dad did put a bid on the van.

3. When will you get the van, Dad?

4. Sid, the kid, hid in the van.

5. Did Mom get rid of that bad lid?

6. Will Pam put a lid on the tan pan?

7. No, she will not put a lid on it.

8. You can put the lid on the pan, Nan!

9. Pat will get the van mid-day, today!

10. The kid hid the pan and the lid.

11. When do you want to get rid of the big rig?

12. Dad wants to get rid of two big rigs today.

13. Mom wants you to put on Kit's wig!

14. Today Dan did a jig with the pals.

15. My pals and I want to play and do a jig.

Lesson 13   _im _ip

Vocabulary Words				Sight Words
dim	rim	Kip	tip	as
him	Tim	lip	zip	so
Jim	dip	rip		said
Kim	hip	sip		were

* See Instructions Page 65.

Sentences

1. Tim will rip the two tan bags.

2. Kim wants to sit at the rim of the pit.

3. Jim can do a jig with his hips.

4. She will sip it with her lips.

5. When will he dip it in the pan?

6. Max does not want to sip it.

7. She said she will zip it, Pat.

8. So, were you at the van at mid-day?

9. Dan will do as he said he will, Dad.

10. Do not tip the cans, Al!

11. Were you mad at Sam today?

12. Yes, I was mad at Sam today.

13. Kim, will you go to the rim with Pat?

14. Did Jim want to have Tim go with him?

15. So, as Jim said, Tim can not go with him today.

Lesson 14   __en __on __un

Vocabulary Words				Sight Words	
Ben	men	on	run	for	about
den	pen	bun	sun	but	be
hen	ten	fun			me
Ken	Don	gun			

✳ See Instructions Page 65.

Sentences

1. Ben wants to run about in the sun with me.

2. About ten men will be in the den with Dad.

3. Ken has said he wants two pigs in his pen.

4. Don and Hal will have fun with Ben's hat.

5. Ben, will you go get the buns for me?

6. She said we can play with Al and Sam at ten.

7. Will you go put this in the den for her?

8. Ken will go play in the sun at two with Jim.

9. What is her name? Is it Jan?

10. No, her name is not Jan. It is Pat.

11. I want to play, but Don does not want to!

12. No, Don is mad, and he will not be fun to play with.

13. Are you about to get into the pen with the two hens?

14. Yes, we are in the pen with the hens.

15. Does that kid have a name?

Lesson 15   __eg __og __ug

Vocabulary Words					Sight Words
beg	dog	jog	dug	lug	began
leg	fog	log	hug	rug	begin
peg	hog	bug	jug	tug	begun
					there

✳ See Instructions Page 65.

Sentences

1. There is a bug on the rug.

2. Tim wants to hug our dog.

3. Kim and Ben want to jog at ten.

4. Ken dug two pits today.

5. Pat began to tug at the peg.

6. Hal has begun to beg for the ham!

7. Will Al begin to play if there is fog today?

8. Nan said she has two logs to play on.

9. Mom said that hog has two bad legs!

10. Can you lug that big jug for me?

11. Pat began to hug the big lad.

12. The hen has begun to play with the hog.

13. Pam, do you want to jog?

14. She wants to run and play with Jim.

Lesson 16 ___et ___ot ___ut

Vocabulary Words					Sight Words
bet	net	cot	lot	cut	down
get	pet	dot	not	hut	out
jet	set	got	pot	jut	why
let	wet	hot	rot	nut	
met	yet	jot	but	rut	

✳ Notice that we are now using the font style for little "a" and "g" that is normally used in published material and computer writing.

✳ Quotation marks (" ") are placed right before and right after the words that someone says to someone else. Example: Jim said to Al, "Go get the pan and lid." Notice that the first word inside the quotation starts with a capital letter.

✳ Also notice that a comma (,) goes before and after a quotation, unless the sentence begins or ends with that quotation.

✳ See Instructions Page 65.

Sentences

1. My bet is that Ben will go down to play with him.

2. Why does the cot get wet in the fog?

3. Jan said, "Pam can not begin to play yet."

4. Hal said, "Dad put a nut in the hot pot."

5. Why did she put the pet in the net?

6. I met Sal at the jet today.

7. Will she let Al set the cot in the hut?

8. Jim got the log and put it out by the rut.

9. You can jot his name down, but not my name.

10. Did Dad put a lot of jam on the ham?

11. Ken will cut the log with his ax.

12. Why will Max set the wick in the wax?

13. "Put the ax down!" said Dad.

14. "You are not to play with an ax," he said.

15. "You do not want to get cut!" Mom said.

16. Dad said to cut it out!

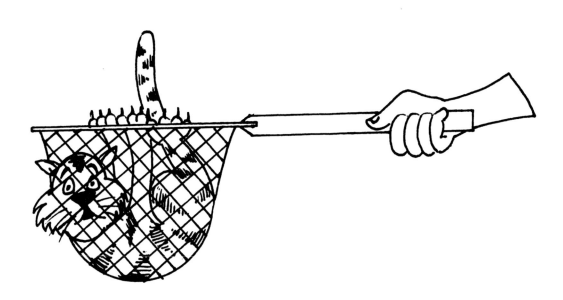

Lesson 17   _d _p

Vocabulary Words					Sight Words
bed	Ted	pod	mop	dud	could
fed	pep	rod	pop	mud	would
led	cod	bop	sop	cup	should
Ned	God	cop	top	pup	
red	nod	hop	bud	up	

✷ See Instructions Page 65.

Sentences

1. Could Ned put the bed in the den?

2. I fed the pup. I put ham in his pan.

3. Would Ted want to put it up on top of his bed?

4. Sam said, "Yes, I want a cup."

5. Al, should you dip the rag down into the mud?

6 Al should not dip the rag down into the mud!

7. Max is not Al's bud, but he is Sam's bud.

8. Why does Kim hop when she mops?

9. I have a lot of pep when I play with my dog, Tab.

10. The lad led his red dog, Tab, down to his hut.

11. Dad said he wants to get a red hot rod.

12. Would you let me get wet in the mud?

13. She would not let me play in the mud.

14. I would get up on top of the bed if I could.

15. I could sop it up with a mop if you would let me.

Lesson 18   _b _x _s _m

Vocabulary Words						Sight Words
web	lob	dub	tub	hem	sum	add
Bob	mob	hub	Rex	Mom	us	your
cob	rob	pub	box	Tom	bus	that
gob	sob	rub	fox	gum	Gus	they
job	cub	sub	ox	hum		them
						says

✻ See Instructions Page 65.

Sentences

1. Mom says that the bug put a web in the tub!

2. Why did Tom put the cub down into the box?

3. The man said, "You should not have gum on my bus!"

4. Gus wants to hum when he plays the sax.

5. Mom, would you fix the hem for me?

6. Tom said, "When you add, you get a sum."

7. Dad will get us an ox to put in the pen.

8. Mom said, "There is a fox in the hen's pen!"

9. I will sob if Mom says, "No, you can not go with them!"

10. "Do not rub the dog's bad leg," said Mom and Dad.

11. It is Max's job to put Tom on the bus today.

12. I want the ox to do his job and lug that box of logs.

13. Bob will not rob you of your pay, so do not say that.

14. They will let you have your gob of gum.

15. When did Bob pay us for the wicks we got for the wax?

Lesson 19   ss, nn, ll, gg, ff, zz, dd

Vocabulary Words						Sight Words
bass	bell	fill	will	cuss	Ann	Mr.
Cass	fell	gill	hiss	fuss	egg	Mrs.
lass	Nell	hill	kiss	Russ	Jeff	Miss
mass	sell	Jill	miss	dull	inn	Ms.
pass	tell	kill	boss	gull	doll	boat
sass	well	mill	loss	hull	odd	
Bess	yell	pill	moss	mull		
less	Bill	sill	Ross	fizz		
mess	dill	till	toss	buzz		

✳ When a word has a double letter, the two letters sound like one letter.

✳ "Mr." is a formal title used before a man's name. "Mrs." is used before a married woman's name. "Miss" is used before a girl or unmarried woman's name, and "Ms." can be used before any woman's name.

✳ See Instructions Page 65.

Sentences

1. Miss Jill is a girl, so she is a lass.

2. Is Miss Nell about to kiss Mr. Bill?

3. Tell Russ to pass the pills to Mrs. Bess.

4. Our cat did not hiss at your two dogs!

5. Do not yell at Jeff! He will get the doll for Ann.

6. Mr. and Mrs. Bell went to the inn for eggs and ham.

7. There is less of a mess in the hull of the boat.

8. Dan did not fuss a lot when he fell down on his bad leg.

9. Nan will sell that odd doll to them if they pay.

10. The pop goes fizz, fizz, fizz!

11. They went to the top of the hill to fill the pan for Ann.

12. There is a gull up there in the fog.

13. Sam and Russ have a dull tin pan to play with.

14. That is odd. The cat did not kill a rat today.

15. Ms. Ann went to the mill to get Mr. Dan.

Lesson 20   _ck

Vocabulary Words					Sight Words
back	tack	lick	hock	Huck	from
hack	Zack	Nick	jock	luck	or
Jack	Beck	pick	lock	muck	then
lack	deck	Rick	mock	puck	where
Mack	neck	sick	rock	tuck	who
pack	peck	tick	sock	yuck	
rack	hick	wick	tock		
sack	kick	dock	duck		

✳ In this lesson, 'ck' sounds just like (k).

✳ Vowels are the letters 'a e i o u'. There are two kinds of vowels, short vowels and long vowels. A short vowel is the sound of the letter that we have learned already from the ABC Sound List and the flash cards. The long sound of a vowel is when it sounds like the name of the letter. The letter 'y' is a vowel when it makes the sound of a vowel. Example: "my," "lucky." The rest of the letters are called consonants.

✳ Here is the rule for using the letters 'ck' instead of the letter 'k'. Use 'ck' after a short vowel.

✳ See Instructions Page 65.

Sentences

1. Mr. Beck will pick Jack and Nick to lock the pen.

2. Mrs. Beck will tell Rick to put the sack on the deck.

3. They went back to the dock where they could pet the ducks.

84

4. Who will pack up the hen's eggs to sell to Mr. Peck?

5. Do not put rocks on the bed or Ms. Huck will be mad.

6. Zack, who said you should put your socks on?

7. We got the tacks from Mack and Mr. Beck.

8. Did Mom kiss you and tuck you into bed?

9. Mack had bad luck when he got hit on the neck.

10. Sal, do not kick that dog or he will get mad!

11. If you pet the dog, he will lick you on the neck.

12. Pam and Jill got sick when they went to the dock.

13. Pick up the box of socks, and then put them there.

14. Where did you get the rocks from?

15. "Rick got that sack of rocks from Jeff," I said.

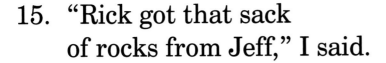

Lesson 21   _st _sk

Vocabulary Words					Sight Words
cast	jest	fist	just	desk	knew
fast	lest	list	must	dusk	know
last	nest	mist	rust	husk	knows
mast	rest	cost	ask	musk	known
past	test	lost	bask	tusk	whose
vast	vest	dust	mask		
best	west	gust	task		

✳ A verb is a word that tells what someone or something <u>does</u>. When 'ed' is added to the end of a verb, it means that something has already happened. Example: John <u>batted</u> the ball.

✳ When 'ing' is added to the end of a word, it means that something is or was happening. Example: John is batting the ball.

✳ A suffix is a letter or letters added to the end of a word which changes the word; 'ed' and 'ing' are suffixes.

✳ Notice in the Sight Words the word "whose." This is tricky because it actually means something belongs to someone. Example: "Whose coat is that?" "Who's" is a contraction that means "who is." Example: "Who's that lady?"

✳ See Instrustions Page 65.

Sentences

1. Sal has known that he must do his best on the test.

2. Pam is the last name on Mrs. Peck's list.

3. I will ask Dad if he knows if we are going west or not.

4. Hal, the ducks are just past the nest.

5. Mom wants to rest, and then she will dust.

6. Whose task is it to get the husks from the pen?

7. Did you know that your fist has mud on it?

8. By dusk the mist should be on the top of the hill.

9. Max has a big, red vest.

10. Does Dad know that there is rust on his van?

11. Mr. Beck has just dusted his tan desk.

12. I want to ask Dot where the ducks are from.

13. Will you tell us whose desk she is sitting at?

14. I know they have begun to do the task.

15. Max knew that if he wanted to win, he would have to go fast.

Lesson 22   _nd _nt

Vocabulary Words					Sight Words
and	fend	pond	rent	mint	any
band	lend	ant	sent	tint	many
hand	mend	can't	tent	bunt	ball
land	send	pants	vent	hunt	came
sand	wind	dent	went	punt	come
end	bond	lent	hint	runt	goes
bend	fond	pent	lint		some
					their

✳ A noun is a word that is a person, place or thing, example: Dad, home, mud. An adjective is a word that gives information about a noun, example: muddy. His pants are muddy. Muddy describes the pants.

✳ When the letter 'y' is added to the end of a word, it makes a sound like the name of the letter 'e'. It can change a word from a noun to an adjective. For example, the word "mud" is a noun. If you add the letter 'y' to "mud" the word becomes "muddy" which is an adjective. When a noun is changed to an adjective by adding a 'y', that adjective describes the noun. For example: "mud" becomes "muddy" meaning that something is like mud or has mud on it. Notice the extra 'd' in "muddy"?

✳ Two words can be put together to form a new word. The new word is called a compound word. The compound word can have an entirely new meaning or it can have the same meaning of the two words put together. Examples: "for" and "get" become "forget" which has a new meaning "to not remember," but "hill and "top" combine to make "hilltop" which means "the top of the hill."

✳ Contractions use an apostrophe (') to show where two words have been brought together and where letters have been left out. Example: "can't" means "can not," and the apostrophe (') shows that the letters 'n' and 'o' have been left out.

✳ See Instructions Page 65.

Sentences

1. When I was sick, Mom sent me off to the tent to rest.

2. Dad hunts for bugs in the mud!

3. When you played ball, did you punt or bunt the ball?

4. Sandy has muddy pants!

5. Did the man bend that big rod with his two hands?

6. The ducks came to their pond to hunt for bugs.

7. Dan will play in the sand, and I will rest in the wind.

8. Our band is not just any band. It is the best band in the land!

9. Did they put mint jam on their ham?

10. Jack is fond of any cat or dog.

11. Should he lend a hand and mend the net?

12. Will you send the rent today?

13. I know that the band can't lend us a hand, so forget it.

14. If Del ripped his pants, he should mend them.

15. Did Dan hint that he wanted us to come to the pond?

Lesson 23

mp, ft, lt, lf, lp, ld, pt, xt, lk, ct

Vocabulary Words					Sight Words
camp	jump	gift	welt	held	all
damp	lump	lift	hilt	kept	here
lamp	mumps	sift	kilt	wept	than
ramp	pump	loft	lilt	next	this
temp	rump	soft	silt	help	see
pomp	daft	tuft	tilt	kelp	
romp	raft	belt	wilt	yelp	
bump	Taft	felt	act	bilk	
dump	waft	melt	elf	milk	
hump	left	pelt	self	silk	

✳ Do not try to explain how the letters at the top of the page sound by themselves. Show students how they sound while sounding out the words.

✳ When the suffix 'er' is added to the end of a word, it means "more." Example: Sentence #15, "bigger" means "more big."

✳ See Instructions Page 65.

Sentences

1. This pump was a gift from Jack and Bob.

2. If the next camp is going to be here, then I will go!

3. Our tent is damp from the fog, and it is yucky.

4. Put the lamp in the tent next to the soft, lumpy bed.

5. Mom knows to go left to get to the dump.

6. Can Rick and Al lift the raft up this hill?

7. The kids want to sift the sand to see what the lumps are.

8. When Dan acts in the play, he lands on his rump!

9. That elf in the act was a bit daft when he kept yelping.

10. The dog yelped when she could not jump off the raft.

11. Here, would you help Nick get the kids some milk?

12. Did you see the black, silk vest on Mr. Taft?

13. I see the stuff was dumped onto the raft and then put on the pond.

14. He kept all the mints for himself and would not let me have some.

15. That man is bigger than me, but he did not help us.

Lesson 24   br, cr, dr, fr, gr, pr, tr

Vocabulary Words					Sight Words
Brad	craft	drug	grill	trim	don't
brag	cramp	drill	grit	trip	won't
brat	drag	Fran	prod	trick	because
brim	drab	frog	prop	trek	think
Bret	drat	Fred	prick	tress	store
crab	drip	Greg	prim	trot	too
cram	drop	grab	print		
crept	drum	grim	trap		
crib	draft	grip	track		
crop	drift	grid	tram		

* The word "too" means "more than it should be," "also," "very," or "in addition." Examples: I ate too many apples. I want to go, too.

* Notice the contractions "don't" and "won't." Just as we saw with "can't" in Lesson 22, "don't" means "do not," and "won't" means "will not."

* See Instructions Page 65.

Sentences

1. Brad, help me, I don't have a grip on the drum!

2. Greg and Fran won't grab the frogs as they jump up.

3. Fred has a grin that is too big.

4. I think that Greg will brag about all the crabs in his trap.

5. Bret and Fran will trot and drop off the pump for Dad.

6. Should Nick drag the log to the ramp on the left?

7. She thinks there is a drip coming down because it is wet there by the pump.

8. When we get sick, Mom has us take our pills from the drug store.

9. Dad, will you put Jimmy down for a nap in his crib?

10. Some think we should trim the fat off the ham.

11. It would be so fun to go on a trip.

12. I don't think Rick is too fond of frogs and crabs.

13. Brad has his cup filled to the brim, and I think it will spill. Don't you think so too?

14. Jill is too ill to go; she has cramps in her legs and back.

15. Whose dog drifted into our camp and left tracks?

Lesson 25   bl, cl, fl, gl, pl, sl

Vocabulary Words					Sight Words
bland	clap	flat	plan	slap	hour
bled	clip	fled	plant	slat	look
blend	Clint	flip	plop	sled	over
blob	clod	flit	plot	slid	how
blog	clog	flint	plug	slim	good
blot	clop	flog	plum	slip	sister
blond	club	flop	plus	slit	
blunt	flab	glad	slab	slop	
clad	flag	gland	slam	slot	
clam	flap	Glen	slant		

✳ See Instructions Page 65.

Sentences

1. We should let Clint flip the sled over to see how flat it is.

2. Glen, don't brag about slamming the clam on the ramp!

3. Bret, did you get a good look at their tricky trap?

4. Fred slid into Clint's fender. Clint got mad, then Fred fled!

5. Do you see the flag flapping in the gusty wind?

6. You put the pigs into the pen as if it was the slammer!

7. Look at the wax as it is plopping down into the jug.

8. Glen thinks we should go slop the hogs with Brent.

9. I want to see Russ flap like a duck.

10. Sid slipped off the dock and then he bled.

11. Did Nell put the plug in the tub?

12. Pam is getting slimmer, and she is glad.

13. Go and blot that spill with the rags.

14. Micky, come on over here to have some plums!

15. Huck said it was drab in the club, and it was cramped, too!

16. My sister is not a brat!

17. She thinks we should blend the milk in a blender for an hour, to get rid of the lumps.

Lesson 26

sc, sk, sm, sn, sp, st, sw, tw

Vocabulary Words					**Sight Words**
scalp	smug	sped	step	twelve	way
scat	smut	spell	stop	twenty	time
scan	snag	spend	stub	twig	boy
scud	snap	spin	swam	twin	girl
skid	snip	spot	swell	twist	okay
skin	snit	spun	swept		
skip	snub	Stan	swift		
skit	snug	stand	swim		
smog	span	stem	swum		

✻ See Instructions Page 65.

Sentences

1. My skin is all muddy from stepping into that bog.

2. It is okay to snap the stems off if you want them to fit into the pot.

3. Stan must swim twenty laps in less than an hour to win the Boys Cup.

4. Miss Fran has a twin named Mr. Stan, and they swam in the pond.

5. I can see the boys and girls spinning!

6. Jim has swum at that spot many times and knows the way to get there.

7. The boys are not just spitting and skipping, they are snapping off the twigs to play with, too.

8. Are the boys and girls willing to stand for two hours?

9. Well, that happy girl is as snug as a bug in a rug.

10. The boys swiftly swept the clump of sand off the tracks.

11. Jill cut a slit in the top of the flap on the box.

12. Hal crammed the stumps of logs he cut down into the back of the van.

13. Nick is being a snob when he snubs the boys and girls.

14. How many times have you snagged that rug?

15. Over the span of twelve hours, he will plan how to win the big trip.

16. Ricky is acting smug because he knows he is winning.

Lesson 27   Multiple Consonant Blends

Vocabulary Words					Sight Words
smell	glass	sniff	track	flock	done
spell	grass	stiff	speck	stock	one
swell	bless	bluff	brick	cluck	use
drill	dress	gruff	click	pluck	again
grill	press	stuff	flick	stuck	against
skill	bliss	scruff	slick	truck	away
spill	floss	black	stick	struck	
still	cross	crack	trick		
brass	staff	smack	block		
class	cliff	snack	clock		

* Consonants are letters that are not vowels. (See Lesson 20)

* Notice that <u>scr</u>uff and <u>str</u>uck have three consonants blended together.

* In sentence #7, the contraction "let's" is a combination of "let" and "us."

* See Instructions Page 65.

Sentences

1. Jack says, "I am still the best one in this class!"

2. Mr. Crab's brass clock goes tick-tock many times an hour.

3. Flint played a trick on Brad, and his truck got stuck in the muck.

4. Ken, can you spell "bliss," "blog" and "grid"?

5. I think Tom should use a stick to get the flock to go away.

6. What stuff do you have here that is good for a snack?

7. Let's go over the drill again and again so we know it.

8. Just pluck your big staff out of the slick mud.

9. When Tom was done helping her, she said, "Bless you."

10. Down the block we could see the boys pressing against the glass of the store.

11. Mom said we should dress up today to go to class.

12. Dan thinks he can stack the many bricks without getting a speck of dust on himself.

13. Mrs. Clopper is skilled at trimming the plants.

14. My hunting dog can sniff tracks up to the bluff!

15. Pam, tell me when you are done pressing the dress.

16. Dad, that is a swell, black, grill you got today at the store.

Lesson 28   ang, ing, ong, ung

Vocabulary Words					Sight Words
bang	bing	bring	dong	hung	like
fang	ding	cling	gong	lung	every
hang	king	fling	Kong	rung	air
rang	ping	sling	long	sung	around
sang	ring	sting	pong	clung	arm
clang	sing	swing	song	stung	water
swang	ting	string	wrong	swung	each
twang	wing	bong	dung	wrung	call

* Notice that <u>str</u>ing has three consonants blended together.

* The word "rung" means "a stout stick, rod, or bar" as in a step on a ladder. It also can mean the past tense of the verb "to ring". Examples: Each step on a ladder is a rung. Mick has rung that bell every day for twenty days!

* Notice that the 'wr' in <u>wr</u>ong sounds like (r), and the 'w' is silent. This is normal.

* Many of the vocabulary words make a sound, like "clang", "twang", "ding", "dong" and "bong".

* As we learned in Lesson 11, a comma can be used with a conjunction (for, and, nor, but, or, yet, so) to join two simple sentences. A semicolon (;) may also be used to join two sentences. For example, see sentence #4.

* See Instructions Page 65.

Sentences

1. Each step on a ladder is a rung.

2. Mick has rung that bell every day for twenty days!

3. When the rag had a lot of water in it, Mom wrung it out.

4. The kids hung around; they like to play ping-pong.

5. The kids ring the bells, and the bells go ding-dong.

6. When a bug with wings stings me, I flick it away!

7. Dad, the kids want to come over to sing songs.

8. Tell Ken to bring a sling to put on Tom's arm.

9. Don't bang on that brass drum; I am sick of it!

10. Jack sang a song with a twang and Tim rang the bell that swung over the deck.

11. When you pick at the string, it will snap and go, "twang."

12. I like to fill my lungs with the good air at camp.

13. Nick has sung that song to Nell about ten times, I think.

14. Al clung to the swing as he swang all day.

15. Why are there so many strings hanging from the net?

16. Why does Kimmy cling to her Mommy so long?

17. That thing looks like a duck up in the air.

Lesson 29 ank, ink, onk, unk

Vocabulary Words					Sight Words
bank	clank	link	drink	junk	army
dank	crank	mink	bonk	sunk	before
Hank	drank	pink	honk	clunk	now
rank	Frank	rink	konk	drunk	head
sank	plank	sink	bunk	skunk	treasure
tank	spank	tink	dunk	trunk	ocean
yank	dink	wink	gunk		floor
blank	ink	clink	hunk		chest

✳ Many of the vocabulary words make a sound, like "clank", "clink", "honk" and "clunk".

✳ We learned in Lesson 22 that when the letter 'y' is added to the end of a word, it makes the word an adjective. In addition, 'en' may be added to the end of a word to make it an adjective. Example: "sunk" becomes "sunken."

✳ When 'ly' is added to the end of the word, the word becomes an adverb and describes an action. Example: "swift" becomes "swiftly" meaning that something is moving in a swift manner.

✳ See Instructions Page 65.

Sentences

1. Why don't we all hang around the rink with Hank?

2. Frank, when you were in the Army, what rank were you?

3. I can see that Bob's skunk has drunk all of Bob's milk.

4. Mom, I would like a drink of water or milk.

5. Dad should stop her from yanking the lamp down now!

6. He winked at me before he dunked me into the tank.

7. Jan, why did you drink all of the milk in the glass jug?

8. Is that a pink stamp you stuck on the box?

9. Is it okay that my trunk has a lot of junk in it?

10. Tom dropped the trunk and it clinked, clanked, and clunked swiftly all the way down the hill.

11. Don't konk me on the head with that clunky bell!

12. When Jeff yanked Frank's hair, Frank got cranky!

13. The sunken treasure chest was at the floor of the ocean.

14. I think it is fun that you have a bunk bed.

15. Do you still want me to bring the cracked bricks to you?

Lesson 30   Contractions   n't

Vocabulary Words			Sight Words
isn't	wasn't	haven't	been
aren't	hasn't	doesn't	ready
couldn't	weren't	mustn't	show
hadn't	shouldn't	wouldn't	year
didn't	don't	won't	John
			night

✱ In Lessons 22 and 24 we learned about contractions. In these contractions, the letters *n't* mean "not". Most contractions have the normal sound for the first word, but notice that "don't" does not have the normal sound of "do" even though it means "do not," and "won't" does not have "will" even though it means "will not."

✱ Notice in sentence #1 that "come" has dropped the silent 'e' when 'ing' is added. The rule is this: if a word ends in an 'e', drop the 'e' if you are adding a suffix that begins with a vowel. For example, the following suffixes begin with vowels: *en, ed, er*, and *ing*.

✱ See Instructions Page 65.

Sentences

1. John isn't coming over here tonight and Nell is so sad.

2. They haven't been ready for years, I think.

3. Flint wasn't thinking, and spilled the wax all over the rug.

4. Dad said they mustn't use the sleds on the bank of the big hill.

5. She thinks we shouldn't go to that show, not yet anyway.

6. We weren't ready for that "gong" in the last act!

7. Frank wasn't ready to help the kids with the task.

8. Aren't you all coming over here for the next show?

9. It's funny that Dad doesn't like to smell a skunk.

10. Pam hasn't swum in the pond for many years.

11. I hadn't been to a show with Bill in twenty years!

12. I don't want Jim to think I am mad at him.

13. For many years Jim wasn't here because of the Army.

14. Couldn't Rick fix the flat on his truck?

15. Glen won't be glad if you are still mad or upset at him.

Lesson 31

Contractions 'd, 'll, 've, 's, 're, 'm

Vocabulary Words				Sight Words
he'd	he'll	I've	who's	people
I'd	I'll	they've	they're	those
she'd	she'll	you've	you're	tomorrow
they'd	they'll	we've	we're	home
we'd	we'll	he's	I'm	baby
you'd	you'll	she's		oh

✳ In these contractions

('d) stands for (would or had)　　('ll) stands for (will)

('s) stands for (is)　　('re) stands for (are)

('ve) stands for (have)　　('m) stands for (am)

Some of the above contractions may also be added to names that we have learned. See sentence #11.

✳ See Instructions Page 65.

Sentences

1. Look at all those people. I know they're happy!

2. We're going to swim in the pond again tomorrow.

3. You're a big boy, Jim, and you'll get bigger next year!

4. We've got to go because she'll be home in a bit.

5. I don't think she should be jumping and skipping with that baby.

6. Do you think they've been to the dock with their boat yet?

106

7. Mr. Taft thinks you've seen the crack in the plank.

8. I'm going to sniff at it to help me know what it is.

9. They'll be home tonight or tomorrow, I think.

10. You'll be here when Mom gets home.

11. She's ready to go, but who's with her? Oh, Tom's with her.

12. John said he'd stack the planks for you.

13. We'd sing twenty songs if you'd let us.

14. Do you think he'll be here by ten?

15. We'll get the job done, you'll see!

16. I think she'll grin when she sees how funny the kids are.

17. I'd like to dunk that dusty rag in the sink of water.

18. They'd put the baby in a crib if they had a crib.

19. I bet you'll press your luck and ask again, won't you?

20. Dot says she'd like to get a backpack for the swim club.

Lesson 32 sh

Vocabulary Words					Sight Words
shall	clash	fresh	shop	mush	other
shack	crash	mesh	shot	rush	another
ash	flash	shin	shock	blush	brother
bash	slash	ship	Josh	flush	mother
cash	smash	shift	posh	slush	father
dash	trash	dish	slosh	brush	hey
gash	shed	fish	shut	crush	snow
lash	shell	wish	gush	shrug	
rash	shelf	swish	hush		
sash	flesh	shod	lush		

✳ When letters 's' and 'h' are put together, they make a completely different sound (sh) which we have seen in "she" and "should." This sound is a digraph, one sound that is made when two letters are put together to make a different sound. This is the first of many digraphs we will learn.

✳ Notice that <u>sh</u>rug has three consonants together which includes the 'sh' digraph.

✳ See Instructions Page 65.

Sentences

1. Hey Tom, did you know my brother, Josh, is on a ship?

2. Mother said that I should put the dishes on the shelf now.

3. Father said we should take the cracked dishes to the trash, but we can't smash them up.

4. Hey John, would you like to go fishing with Father?

5. I am rushing! I wish another bus was coming for us.

6. Hey boys, shall we dash to the shed to get the brush?

7. When the snow melts, we'll have a lot of slush around.

8. Put your shells in the shed, then shut and lock it.

9. Hey girls, do you have any pink blush for me to use?

10. That man just dashed out of the store and ran with the cash!

11. That ball hit his shin, and I think he's in shock!

12. Let's rush and shift our tent to the other camp!

13. Don't forget to brush well, and swish around with water.

14. Did you see Dan's red rash on his arms and legs?

15. She should flush the pills down with milk or water.

16. If you crush the bug, it will become a yucky blob.

17. When the vat cracked, melted wax gushed out.

18. Did Mrs. Beck fix a dish of fresh fish?

19. Del said he'd be back in a flash, but I don't see him yet.

Lesson 33 th

Vocabulary Words				Sight Words	
thank	thin	fifth	broth	cry	fly
bath	think	sixth	sloth	dry	sly
path	thing	Smith	thud	try	fry
Beth	thrill	with	thump	sky	shy
tenth	thick	moth	thrust		

✳ When the letters 't' and 'h' are put together, they make a completely different sound, 'th'. Remember, this is called a digraph. We have seen the 'th' sound already in the words "the," "then," "that," and "their."

✳ In these Sight Words, the 'y' makes a sound that we call a "long i" sound. We have already seen the "long i" sound in the words "like" and "time." In these Sight Words the "long i" sound is not made with an 'i', but with the letter 'y'.

✳ See Instructions Page 65.

Sentences

1. For the sixth time, Beth is going to try to fly in thick fog.

2. If you thump the glass jug on the floor, it will make a thud.

3. Mrs. Smith thinks Beth is going to cry if she gets stung.

4. Miss Jill slid on the thin ramp for the fifth time.

5. That girl is so shy she blushes when Lester talks to her.

6. Dad wants you to dry off when you get out of the bath tub.

7. I am so glad you'll fry eggs for us today, Mrs. Smith.

8. When you're on the path at the top of the hill, at dusk, look up in the sky and you'll see the sun going down.

9. For the tenth time, what is that thing over there?

10. If we do our tasks, Dad will be glad and thank us.

11. Bring baby Tim over tomorrow night, and I'll babysit him so you two can go to the show.

12. I've been trying for some time to think of a sly plan.

13. Hasn't Mr. Smith been drinking the water from his well?

14. I'll bet the kids picked those plums against John's wish.

15. Thank you for helping me.

Lesson 34   ch

Vocabulary Words				Sight Words
Chad	chop	chant	lunch	please
chap	chug	chest	munch	after
chat	chum	inch	punch	excuse
Chet	chill	pinch	stench	very
chin	chick	ranch	wrench	
chip	check	bench	such	
chit	Chuck	bunch	rich	

Instructions

✳ When the letters 'c' and 'h' are put together, they make a completely different sound, 'ch', which is another digraph.

✳ Notice that the 'wr' in <u>wr</u>ench sounds like (r), and the 'w' is silent. This is the way 'wr' always sounds.

✳ See Instructions Page 65.

1. Excuse me, Chuck, but isn't Chip your best chum?

2. After the show, Chip will talk with Jill.

3. Hey John, please tell that chap, "Chill out!"

4. It was funny to see Sam's punch dripping from his chin down to his chest!

5. Let's have a bunch of people over for a good lunch!

6. You'd better not chug down too much of that punch!

7. We had such a good chat with those Army people tonight.

8. I think we'll get to go to their ranch today or tomorrow.

9. Did he pinch Chip to get him to stop bugging him?

10. Let's chop up all the logs so we can use them at camp.

11. Can you tell that Mr. and Mrs. Smith are very rich?

12. Max will sit on the bench as his mom goes shopping.

13. Will you please let me pick up the baby chick?

14. As dusk fell, a chill in the air struck me.

15. I don't think Chuck will like you plotting to trick him!

Lesson 35   tch

Vocabulary Words				Sight Words
batch	fetch	pitch	Dutch	hear
catch	sketch	snitch	clutch	work
latch	stretch	switch	crutch	door
match	itch	notch		need
patch	stitch	botch		seem
snatch	ditch	crotch		Holland
				strong

✱ When the letters 't', 'c' and 'h' are put together as 'tch', they make the same sound as 'ch'. Three letters that make one sound are called a "trigraph."

✱ See Instructions Page 65.

Sentences

1. If you need that stick, get your dog to fetch it for you.

2. Nell is going to use a crutch.

3. That man is from Holland; that means he is "Dutch."

4. I have been working all day digging ditches. Now I'll fetch a drink of good, fresh water from our well.

5. Doesn't it seem like it's time for those chicken eggs to hatch?

6. Please go latch that door, for now it is nighttime.

7. Mom, will you please patch my ripped pants?

8. The boy was clutching the brass ship.

9. Here, catch the belt as I toss it to you!

10. That's a very good sketch you did of Miss Hull.

11. Boy, can he pitch fast! Look at his strong arm!

12. Does your back itch because of the rash? Then scratch it.

13. Don't forget to pack a box of matches for camp.

14. You need to switch to the other van; it has more gas in it.

15. Did you hear Dad? He said to get your work done!

Lesson 36   wh, qu

Vocabulary Words				Sight Words	
wham	which	quell	quick	cake	give
whack	whiff	quench	quilt	make	more
when	whisk	quit		take	yesterday
whip	quack	quiz		gave	

* When the letters 'w' and 'h' are put together, it sounds like a 'w'; this is a digraph. Note: this sound used to be taught that 'wh' sounded like there was an 'h' in front of the 'w', but now it is commonly pronounced as (w). However, it is still considered a digraph due to this alternative pronunciation.

* In the English language, the letter 'q' always has the letter 'u' after it, and they make the sound (kw), a digraph.

* In the Sight Words, the words "make," "take," and "gave" have a sound that we call a "long a" sound. We have already seen this "long a" sound in the words "name" and "way."

* See Instructions Page 65.

Sentences

1. They should make a quick switch in the stitching they are using for the quilt.

2. It's best to use a whisk to mix the stuff in that tin pot.

3. Yesterday I quit my job because my boss said he wouldn't pay me.

4. Did you take a whiff of that fresh cut grass?

5. Which quiz are you getting ready for?

6. That baby duck quacks for his mother all of the time.

7. Please tell Frank that it is time to whip up the cake batter.

8. John whacked the big rock with a stick.

9. Wham! The wind slammed the door shut.

10. Would you please look over your quiz one more time before you give it to me?

11. Mom gave her a look that said, "Don't try it!"

12. Yesterday we worked more on the patch quilt we are making for grandmother.

13. Do not give your mother any sass!

14. Mom, will you please get us some more milk?

15. Whose van crashed last night?

Lesson 37   ee

Vocabulary Words					Sight Words
bee	heed	cheek	deep	squeeze	saw
Dee	need	deem	Jeep	sneeze	move
fee	seed	seem	keep	cheese	love
Lee	teed	seen	peep	fifteen	sure
see	weed	screen	seep	sixteen	together
tee	freed	green	weep	cheer	
wee	speed	queen	creep	deer	
free	tweed	beet	sheep	heel	
tree	beef	feet	sleep	feel	
three	reef	meet	sweep	reel	
speech	peek	street	geese	wheel	
deed	seek	sweet	breeze		
feed	week	beep	freeze		

* When two 'e' letters are put together, they usually make the sound of the name of letter 'e,' also called a "long e" sound.

* Notice that on the last column before the sight words, there is a group of words that have a silent 'e' after the 's' or 'z'. Example: "geese" and "breeze."

* The word "cheese" is tricky. The letter 's' sounds like (z) in "breeze."

* See Instructions Page 65.

Sentences

1. I saw fifteen wee baby chicks feeding with their mother.

2. It sure seems like the queen is very glad to meet everyone on the street! The people here sure do love her.

3. Do you see the three lovely green trees that are next to us?

4. My twin baby brothers are asleep together in their crib.

5. Do you feel a need to put your heels up when you nap?

6. Is there such a thing as a sixteen-wheel truck?

7. The deer fed together on the sweet, fresh beets those people gave them.

8. Don't move! Mom dropped a pin over there by your feet!

9. Feel free to look around the ranch; I'm sure you'll find some things those people left.

10. Cheer up! We will pick the weeds that don't belong here.

11. Bobby kissed my cheek, then gave a speech about his love!

12. I was thrilled when my feet went into the deep, hot water.

13. Did Dad put a screen on the door to keep out the bugs?

14. Mom asked you to sweep the rug; why do you sit and weep?

15. Do you feel the breeze coming in off the pond?

16. I love that cheese Mom got!

17. There are fifteen or sixteen geese flying over us in the sky.

18. I'm sure I will freeze in this wind.

Lesson 38 ea

Vocabulary Words				Sight Words	
pea	neat	cream	weave	eager	better
sea	seat	dream	leave	beaver	might
tea	treat	steam	meal	eagle	little
flea	bean	scream	real	breathe	until
lead	Dean	stream	seal	season	since
read	Jean	beach	ear	reason	
leaf	lean	peach	clear	easy	
weak	mean	reach	fear		
eat	clean	teach	hear		
beat	beam	beast	tear		
heat	ream	feast	year		
meat	team	least	beard		

* When the letters 'e' and 'a' are added together, they usually make the sound of the name of the letter 'e', just like 'ee.' This is another digraph.

* Note that some words have multiple pronunciations. For example, the word "tear," "read," and "lead" each have additional pronunciations that have different meanings. Do not confuse your student with these other pronunciations, but if she asks, explain that some words have different pronunciations and different meanings.

* Notice in sentence #15 the word "easy" has changed the 'y' to 'i' before adding the 'ly'.

* See Instructions Page 65.

Sentences

1. We love going to the beach and feasting on fresh peaches and cream.

2. Are you eager to go with us on a steamship out to sea?

3. I had a dream about an eagle with a meal in its nest!

4. At least the little stream looks very clean this season.

5. What is the reason the beaver beats the water?

6. Mr. Bean has been sick for two seasons; therefore, he is now very weak and lean.

7. This is the season dogs get fleas.

8. My mother loves to teach people to read.

9. The seals are eager to eat fresh fish from the sea.

10. Our team is leading the others!

11. I saw the little baby eagle reach for the meal.

12. Oh dear, Mom says we are out of tea!

13. It has been years since I've seen Jean.

14. Jack needs to clean out his ears until he can hear better.

15. John cannot breathe easily because the disease left him weak.

Lesson 39 oo

Vocabulary Words				Sight Words	
boo	spoon	shoot	stool	while	all
goo	boom	coop	food	often	ball
moo	room	goop	roof	made	call
too	bloom	hoop	tooth	always	fall
zoo	broom	loop	goose	silly	hall
boon	boot	whoop	loose		mall
goon	coot	scoop	choose		small
loon	hoot	cool	rooster		tall
moon	root	fool	igloo		wall
noon	toot	tool			
soon	loot	spool			

✳ Here is another digraph, "oo", where two letters put together have a different sound.

✳ Notice the silent letter 'e' at the end of "goose," "loose," and "choose." Notice that "loose" and "goose" have a soft (s) sound at the end, but the 's' in "choose" sounds like (z).

✳ In the Sight Words, the words ending in "all" have a sound we have already heard in the words "all," "ball," and "call."

✳ See Instructions Page 65.

Sentences

1. Will we always see a goose and a rooster at the zoo?

2. In the meantime, Miss Reed will shoot the hoops.

3. It is cool tonight, and the moon is a lovely, small ball.

4. Soon I will sweep the bedroom with the tall broom.

5. I often trip on the roots and fall while working in the backyard.

122

6. A spoon is a handy tool to help us eat food.

7. At noon the rooster sits on the roof and munches on his food.

8. Oh my, one tooth is cracked and another is loose!

9. Which hoop are you going to shoot the ball into?

10. Some people eat and sleep in igloos.

11. What did she put around the spool?

12. Are you going to hoot, toot and whoop it up at midnight?

13. Does Mr. Meed always sit and spin on that stool like that?

14. Sometimes I choose to act silly and have fun!

15. Oh dear, did you hear the boom the van made when it hit the wall?

16. Hey, let's all go to the mall and look at the shops.

17. Call me when you are done cleaning the rugs in the halls.

Lesson 40   oo

Vocabulary Words				Sight Words	
book	nook	crook	stood	under	grandma
cook	rook	shook	foot	most	grandpa
hook	took	good	wool	house	side
look	brook	wood	cookie	Sharon	China

✱ In this lesson, two 'o' letters put together have a different sound. Now they sound like the (u) in the word "put." We have seen this sound before in the word "look."

✱ See Instructions Page 65.

Sentences

1. We will need most of the wood to heat the house this season.

2. I would love to have a yummy cookie while I sit at home and read a good book.

3. Jim took all of the rugs out and shook them very well.

4. Sharon saw the ranchers shear the wool from the sheep.

5. The cook stood on one foot while he cooked, just to have fun. Miss Reed thinks the cook is silly.

6. The shy, black cat is under the woodshed.

7. I think that Jean took most of the good books home.

8. Dad's beard looks like a bunch of wool on his chin.

9. Oh Sharon, please make a pot of your good sun tea for us!

10. Mom, I saw brother take some cookies when you said not to; he ran under the house with them!

11. He shook his foot to get most of the mud off.

12. Are you all ready? I want us to go soon.

13. Hank saw the crook run out of the bank with the loot.

14. Grandma has a little nook where she keeps her old china dishes.

15. Grandpa and I like to go fishing in the brook that runs alongside his farm.

Lesson 41   Suffix ed

Vocabulary Words					Sight Words
bat	end	lift	nod	hunt	son
batted	ended	lifted	nodded	hunted	ago
sag	spell	fill	rob	stub	toe
sagged	spelled	filled	robbed	stubbed	minute
help	ask	fix	drop	brush	answer
helped	asked	fixed	dropped	brushed	

✷ As we learned in Lesson 21, when 'ed' is added to the end of a word, it means it has already happened. Notice that there are three different sounds of 'ed': (ed), (d) or (t). The sound to use depends on the last sound of the word to which it is attached. Listen to the ending as you say the words.

✷ See Instructions Page 65.

Sentences

1. Would Jack like to hunt with the rest of the men?

2. No, he stubbed his toe badly, yesterday.

3. When Nan gives her answer, she will nod her head.

4. Nan already nodded her head, didn't you see?

5. Could you lift that big box of wood for Mr. Sam?

6. I lifted the box awhile ago for him, and he's happy.

7. Mom said she wants you to end that show now!

8. She need not get upset; I already ended it a minute ago.

9. Is Mrs. Jean's son going to bat next?

10. No, Mrs. Jean's son batted three minutes ago, silly!

11. Why don't you tag me next?

12. What do you mean? I tagged you awhile ago.

13. Will you spell a word for me?

14. I just spelled six words for you.

15. Sally filled her cup with too much milk. It's going to spill onto her foot!

16. That man robbed the bank, and I saw him do it!

17. The girls asked the boys to fix lunch this time.

18. Who dropped the glass lamp on his food?

19. She already brushed her teeth ten minutes ago.

Lesson 42   Suffix es, s

Vocabulary Words				Sight Words
hatch	mix	buzz	box	hope
hatches	mixes	buzzes	boxes	flower
press	bat	dog	fox	sneaky
presses	bats	dogs	foxes	between
egg	home			page
eggs	homes			right

✳ As we learned in Lesson 5, sometimes when an 's' is added to a word, it means more than one. The suffix 'es' is added instead of 's' to words ending in 'x,' 'ch,' 'sh,' and 's' to show more than one, or "plural."

✳ Sometimes 's' and 'es' are added to a verb to change how the word is used. Example: catch, catches; jump, jumps. The general rule is this: Add 's' to a verb when it refers to one person or thing, but not "you" or "I." Examples: John <u>sings</u> well. Mary <u>sings</u> well. Mary and John <u>sing</u>. I <u>sing</u> well. You <u>sing</u> well. Mom and Dad <u>sing</u> well.

✳ Notice the sight word "sneaky" has the suffix 'y' on the word "sneak."

✳ See Instructions Page 65.

Sentences

1. How many dogs do you have at your home?

2. We have just one dog.

3. I think cats are sneaky. Do you agree?

4. My cat is very sweet, but he is still tricky.

5. That pink pig is not as fat as those dogs.

6. I used to think that all pigs were fat, but that's not right.

7. I would like you to give me one box, if you can.

8. Well, I was planning to give you two boxes!

9. I really hope that the egg hatches today.

10. The egg will hatch when it is ready.

11. Mom presses the flowers between book pages.

12. I am sure she will press them today after we eat.

13. Do you like to mix up the punch?

14. No, Pam always mixes up the punch for us.

15. He should buzz that bell when he is done.

16. I know, but he always buzzes it too soon.

Lesson 43 Suffix er

Vocabulary Words				Sight Words
bat	send	mix	stop	money
batter	sender	mixer	stopper	noise
catch	lend	pick	hop	draw
catcher	lender	picker	hopper	talk
gush	buzz			walk
gusher	buzzer			

✳ As we learned in Lesson 23, 'er' is a suffix that can mean "more" of something. When 'er' is added to an action word (a verb), it becomes a word that refers to *someone* or *something* who is doing the action (a noun). Example: if you add 'er' to the verb "catch," it becomes "catcher" which means someone who catches.

✳ A syllable is a word, or part of a word, that has one vowel sound. The word "mix" has the sound of one vowel; therefore it is one syllable. The word "mixer" has two separate vowel sounds, first in 'mix' and again in 'er'; therefore, "mixer" has two syllables.

✳ Notice the word "money" in the sight words. When a word ends with 'ey' it usually makes the sound of the name of the letter (e).

✳ See Instructions Page 65.

Sentences

1. Who will be the next kid to bat?

2. Sharon will walk up and be the next batter.

3. Will you lend me some money? Please talk to me.

4. No, Dad will be your lender this time.

5. Do you boys like to box?

6. Yes, but we are not as good as Tim; he's a good boxer!

7. How do you make that buzzing noise?

8. I just press this buzzer right here.

9. Will you help me while I draw a sketch of that cliff?

10. Sure, I will be glad to be your helper.

11. The next time we play, can I be the pitcher or catcher?

12. While we were picking plums, Mommy told little Johnny, "You are a good plum picker!"

13. To stop the water from leaving, put the stopper in the sink.

14. Oh wow! The well they drilled is really a gusher!

Lesson 44   Ending er

Vocabulary Words				Sight Words
matter	better	liver	clutter	thought
scatter	letter	river	stutter	safe
shatter	ever	shiver	summer	lemon
banner	never	silver	supper	favorite
manner	copper	bother	rubber	metal
gather	proper	September	hunger	
rather	bitter	butter	anger	
ladder	litter	gutter	finger	
after				

✻ While we have seen 'er' as a suffix, these words are different. They just end in 'er.'

✻ Sometimes we call a "syllable" a "chunk"; both words refer to a word or part of a word that has a vowel sound. Example: "talking" has 2 syllables: 'talk' and 'ing'. "September" has 3 syllables, 'Sep', 'tem', 'ber'. Some people "clap" to find out how many syllables there are in a word. You clap for every chunk you hear. You would clap only once when saying the word "soft." But you would clap twice while saying the word "soft-ly."

✻ See Instructions Page 65.

Sentences

1. Why don't you gather up all the letters Ben has sent you to put away for safe-keeping?

2. Kids, be sure to mind your manners at Mrs. Smith's home.

3. Please go get the ladder so we can put up the banner.

4. The lemons are even more bitter than I thought they would be.

5. What is your favorite metal, copper or silver?

6. Son, you should never, ever, jump into that deep river without a proper vest on, for it is not safe to do so.

7. This summer we have been making our butter from the cream we get at the top of the milk.

8. Oh dear, you have cluttered up your room with all of your little rubber balls!

9. The robber came into the store and stuttered, "Give m-m-me all your m-m-money!"

10. Dear, after supper please shut all of the shutters.

11. What is the matter? Why are you shivering like that?

12. He has a lot of anger pent up because of how he was treated.

13. I thought her hunger was because she didn't eat for three days.

14. Put your finger on the work you need help with.

15. Our mother cat had a litter of baby kittens in September!

Lesson 45   Suffix er, est, ness

Vocabulary Words					Sight Words
happy	fresh	sad	sick	gruff	guess
happier	fresher	sadder	sicker	gruffer	million
happiest	freshest	saddest	sickest	gruffest	dollar
happiness	freshness	sadness	sickness	gruffness	great
big	hot	some	good		aunt
bigger	hotter	more	better		uncle
biggest	hottest	most	best		

* The "root word" is the original base word to which we can add prefixes and suffixes. We learned in Lesson 23 that when 'er' is added to a root word, it can mean "more" of it. When 'est' is added to a word, it means the "most" of it. When 'ness' is added, then we are talking about the root word in relation to something. For example, "sad" is the root word for "sadder," which means "more sad." "Saddest" means "most sad." "Sadness" has to do with being sad.

* Notice that some words do not change in this way. Example: we say "good," "better," and "best," (not good, gooder and goodest).

* Notice how a two-syllable word that ends with (y) changes when a vowel is added in a suffix. The (y) changes to (i); for example, "happy" becomes "happier."

* Happiness has 3 syllables: 'hap', 'pi', 'ness'.

* See Instructions Page 65.

Sentences

1. Are you sad that Uncle Zack's dog got hit by a car?

2. Yes, I am sad, but I'm sure you are sadder because you really knew the dog.

3. That's right, but I guess that Uncle Zack has got to be the saddest of us all, because it was his dog!

4. I don't feel happy talking about all of this sadness.

5. I got sick from being on the ship out at sea for three days.

6. I got sicker than you; I had to go to bed for two days.

7. Really? Well, I guess Mr. Smith got the sickest of all, because he has been in bed for a week!

8. Yuck, just talking about all this sickness makes me not feel well again.

9. Are you happy that Aunt Sally got a million dollars?

10. I sure am happy, but Aunt Sally's mother is even happier than I am.

11. You can be sure of it, but I guess that Aunt Sally has got to be the happiest one of all, since she has the money!

12. It is more fun to be happy than to be sad.

13. I would like Dad to give me ten dollars.

14. You would? I would like more money, maybe fifteen dollars.

15. Oh? Why don't we ask him for the most, about twenty dollars?

16. Mom said I did a good job making my bed, but I could do better. I guess she's right.

17. You should do the best you can; then everyone will be happy.

Lesson 46 Suffix y, ly, ily

Vocabulary Words					Sight Words
dad	fresh	sick	Bob	pup	woman
daddy	freshly	sickly	Bobby	puppy	women
					Robert
sad	hill	swift	quick	happy	Vera
sadly	hilly	swiftly	quickly	happily	Eric
					drive
				sloppy	
				sloppily	

✷ Sometimes when a 'y' is added to a word it is just a name. Example: a person with the name "Bob" may also be called "Bobby."

✷ As we learned in Lesson 29, when 'ly' is added to the end of the word, the word becomes an adverb and describes the action. Example: "swift" becomes "swiftly" meaning that something is moving in a swift manner.

✷ When a word already ends with a 'y', then the 'y' changes to 'i' before 'ly' is added. Example: "happy" becomes "happily."

✷ Some words become plural, meaning more than one, in an unusual way. "Woman" refers to one adult girl, and "women" refers to more than one.

✷ See Instructions Page 65.

Sentences

1. When Eric was small, he called his father "Daddy."

2. But when Eric got bigger, he called him "Dad."

3. His real name is Robert, but we call him "Bob" or "Bobby."

4. Vera's family has to drive up that hill everyday to get home.

5. The women in our class like to jog swiftly each day.

6. I can tell that Kim is a sad woman. She walks sadly along the path with her pup.

7. Most people love to smell freshly cut flowers.

8. How swift is the water in the river moving?

9. Well, look how swiftly that raft is going downstream.

10. I see that when you run, you sure are quick.

11. Thank you, I like to run quickly.

12. Little Eric is happily singing a song because his mother, Vera, said she loves him, and kissed him on his cheek.

13. Why is that woman so sloppy?

14. I don't know, but did you see how sloppily she put the dishes on the shelf?

Lesson 47   y, ies, ied

Vocabulary Words					Sight Words
empty	copy	study	try	cry	school
empties	copies	studies	tries	cries	Katie
emptied	copied	studied	tried	cried	hard
					Kentucky
family	enemy		fry	fly	Brittney
families	enemies		fries	flies	Alice
			fried	flew	almost
busy	hurry				sorry
busies	hurries		lullaby	satisfy	angry
busied	hurried		lullabies	satisfies	hunger
busily	hurriedly			satisfied	

✳ Just as we saw with 'ly' in Lesson 46, if a word ends with a 'y' the 'y' must be changed to 'i' before adding 'es' or 'ed'.

✳ Notice the unusual change in pattern for "fly," "flies," and "flew."

✳ See Instructions Page 65.

Sentences

1. Dad said, "Eric, empty the trash cans after dinner!"

2. Eric answered, "I already emptied them awhile ago!"

3. Eric empties the trash cans almost every day.

4. My mother always sang me a lullaby before I went to bed.

5. You know, Katie studies hard for every test in school.

6. Katie studied for six hours for that big math test!

7. Hey Dad, did you have any enemies when you were a kid?

8. No, Robert, I did not have any enemies, but there was one kid who was mean to me.

9. My family has worked in metal shops for years.

10. We haven't had food today. I am so hungry!

11. Aunt Alice, I am sorry that I dropped the dish. Are you angry?

12. Brittney, please make some copies of this for me.

13. Uncle Zack is the hardest worker of all those men.

14. Micky and Frank are heading to school right now.

15. Aunt Pam was satisfied with the housework I did for her.

16. Look at the way Aunt Sally busies herself at work.

17. Uncle John flew here from Kentucky.

18. If that food is fried, then Aunt Jill won't eat it.

19. The lovely sketch that Aunt Pat made is now dry.

Lesson 48   en ie ies ied

Vocabulary Words					Sight Words
fat	red	stiff	rot	sunk	hurt
fatten	redden	stiffen	rotten	sunken	both
					eye
Allen	Helen	bitten	gotten	sudden	old
happen	seven	kitten	oxen		fortune
		mitten			watch
die	lie	linen	tie		friend
dies	lies	chicken	ties		story
died	lied	children	tied		
		kitchen			

* Notice the pattern of 'ie' words above. Here, 'ie' sounds like the name of the letter 'i'.

* Remember, in Lesson 29 we learned that 'en' may be added to the end of a word to mean 'to make more like the root word.' Some of the Words above use the suffix 'en' with a root word. Examples: "fatten," "stiffen," and "rotten," .

* Other Vocabulary Words have 'en' as a part of the main, root word. Examples: "happen," "seven," "kitten," "mitten," "linen," "oxen," and "sudden."

* See Instructions Page 65.

Sentences

1. If you don't water the flowers, they will die.

2. Seth is sorry he lied about the homework.

3. Aunt Alice tied the strings of my hat under my chin.

4. Something got into my eye, and it hurts.

5. The kitten has bitten that small kid.

6. Watch the skin redden where the bee stung her.

7. Grandfather said to cook it until it stiffens.

8. Did you know that more than one ox is called oxen?

9. I hear that our friend, Allen, has spent a fortune on a chicken ranch and plans to let his children run it.

10. Grandmother uses a lovely linen cloth at dinner time.

11. Was Uncle Jeb's story about old sunken treasure?

12. Let's go to the kitchen to cook up something to eat.

13. Miss Helen is my mom's favorite older friend.

14. Uncle Ben says we need to fatten up the pig to sell.

15. It seems that big Al has gotten skinny all of a sudden.

16. What happens next to the children in the story?

17. It smells like that food is rotten!

Lesson 49　　_le

Vocabulary Words				Sight Words	
candle	bobble	ample	humble	bottle	month
handle	cobble	sample	crumble	throttle	special
bundle	gobble	trample	mumble	uncle	wonderful
middle	hobble	sprinkle	tumble	bungle	horse
fiddle	pickle	twinkle	grumble	jungle	carry
riddle	tickle	shamble	stumble		carries
saddle	simple	bumble	tremble		
pebble	apple	fumble	little		

✱ The letters 'le' at the end of a word sounds like (ul) as we have already seen with the word "little."

✱ See Instructions Page 65.

Sentences

1. Please don't mumble when you talk. I can't understand you very well.

2. My uncle is a wonderful man with a twinkle in his eye.

3. My grandmother loves to eat pickles.

4. Last month my friend made her special apple pie and we all gobbled it up.

5. I fell against the desk and made the little bottle tumble.

6. My grandfather is a humble old man who trembles as he carries his bundle of wood to the woodshed.

7. Hey Nick, try to put the saddle on the middle of the horse's back.

8. I have never been to a jungle before; this is great!

9. A little rock is called a pebble.

10. We have ample time to sprinkle the seeds for the grass.

11. If you keep on tickling me, I will get mad!

12. I like the way he handles that horse.

13. Don't tremble too much as you carry the lit candle.

14. My uncle carries his children when it's muddy on the path.

15. Middle and riddle are funny words to hear.

16. If you keep grumbling, then you won't get any cookies.

Lesson 50   _el, _al

Vocabulary Words				Sight Words
gavel	nickel	metal	animal	only
gravel	signal	medal	several	warm
travel	pummel	petal	hospital	bought
camel	tunnel	pedal	capital	hold
flannel	funnel	level		Paul
				movie

✳ The letters 'el' and 'al' at the end of words have the same sound of (ul) that we saw in Lesson 49 with the letters 'le'.

✳ See Instructions Page 65.

Sentences

1. For the next several hours, we will be traveling on a gravel road, which is made of pebbles smashed into sand.

2. I think there is a tunnel up ahead; do you see the flashing signal?

3. I wish I had a nickel for every time you said, "Just a minute!"

4. You are going to love the flannel sheets I bought for our beds. They will keep us warmer at night!

5. You had better hold the cup level, or you might spill the milk Mom just put in there.

6. My Uncle Jim is a wonderful man, and he was given a medal for his work in the Army.

7. Jack needs to pedal faster if he wants to get to the movie on time.

8. It is rather odd to see a metal door on a wooden house.

9. I like to smell the petals on those lovely, red flowers.

10. Isn't it great to have animals for pets?

11. When people get very sick, they might need to go to a hospital.

12. Uncle Paul says that some camels have one hump on their backs and others have two humps.

13. There are several movies that I don't want to see!

14. I only have three nickels left; what can I get with them?

15. If you save your nickels for a long time, you will have a small fortune.

145

Lesson 51   _in, _on, _ain

Vocabulary Words				Sight Words	
napkin	cannon	melon	captain	load	brave
pumpkin	dragon	person	chaplain	pie	believe
muffin	gallon	ribbon		wow	pull
Robin	lemon	wagon		beautiful	

✳ When the letters 'on', 'in', or 'ain' are at the end of a word, they sound like (in) or (un).

✳ As we learned in Lesson 5, an apostrophe and the letter 's' ('s) at the end of a word shows that something belongs to it (a possession). If the word already has an 's' sound at the end, then only an apostrophe needs to be added to show possession. For example, "Mr. Smith's hat" is referring to the hat of Mr. Smith, while "the Smiths' horse" in sentence #1 is referring to the horse that belongs to the Smiths.

✳ See Instructions Page 65.

Sentences

1. The Smiths' horse is going to pull that wagon-load of melons from their ranch to the store.

2. Dad went to the store and spent twenty dollars getting two gallons of milk, a bag of lemons, and a pumpkin pie!

3. Wow, Robin has been named the captain of his team!

4. My three brothers are chaplains in the Army.

5. I really believe that is a dragon, and it's going to eat me up!

6. Feel free to use some napkins to clean up that spill.

146

7. Wow, that old treasure ship has real cannons, which can still shoot!

8. Johnny gets happy when he hears that Aunt Helen will bring her wonderful pumpkin pies for dinner.

9. Who around here can make a dragon outfit so that Nick can get dressed up for the special play?

10. Captain Jack will lead the ship's brave men out to sea.

11. One of my favorite foods is soft, tangy, lemon muffins.

12. Oh, look at those beautiful pink and red ribbons!

13. You will get your answer on the next page.

14. Dad thinks Mom is brave to shop at the mall today.

15. Mom is thrilled because the rest of our family is coming home this month!

Lesson 52   _et, _it, _ic, _ish

Vocabulary Words					Sight Words
bucket	pocket	socket	visit	finish	kind
comet	puppet	ticket	fantastic	punish	tiny
docket	trumpet	planet	picnic	selfish	toy
Janet	rocket	rabbit	traffic	foolish	car

✳ When 'et' is at the end of a word, it sounds like (et) or (it).

✳ See Instructions Page 65.

Sentences

1. I hope we don't get a traffic ticket for speeding, Janet!

2. Oh, the children are going to love seeing the rabbits in the fantastic puppet show tomorrow night.

3. Was that a rocket or a comet we just saw up in the sky?

4. Oh Dad, can our family have a picnic at the beach today?

5. Yes, if everyone finishes all their work, we will go at noon, and we'll go to our favorite spot by the dock!

6. If you are right and Tom did stuff all that money in his pocket, then he will be punished.

7. Oh come on, Alice, don't be so selfish. Give us some of the lemons and apples from your wonderful trees!

8. I believe Dan's arm was pulled out of its socket when he fell off of the speeding truck! Now he's going to the hospital.

9. You don't need an excuse to ask; we would love for you to come over and visit any time!

10. I have seen Mom clean the sinks and tubs with a cleaner in a bucket.

11. Little Timmy puts all kinds of things in his pockets, like tiny round balls, frogs, string and tiny, metal toy cars.

12. Get that bucket for me, please; I need to mop the floors in the kitchen and bathrooms.

13. We all guessed right; Frank is from another planet!

14. Is that a real rabbit or a stuffed, toy rabbit?

15. Thanks Dad, for the fantastic tickets you got for us today.

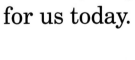

Lesson 53   _ful

Vocabulary Words					Sight Words
thank	meaning	fist	box	cup	bake
thankful	meaningful	fistful	boxful	cupful	chocolate
hope	thought	rest	will	use	own
hopeful	thoughtful	restful	willful	useful	

✷ When the suffix 'ful' is at the end of the word, it means that it is full of the root word. For example, "thankful" means full of thanks.

✷ See Instructions Page 65.

Sentences

1. I am so thankful that those kind people gave a boxful of food to the needy family next door.

2. My Aunt Katie loves to bake cakes and muffins, and she always puts a cupful of creamy milk in the batter.

3. Wasn't that very thoughtful of Mr. Sutton to watch the kids while Mrs. Sutton went shopping at the mall?

4. It was a very meaningful act of love when Dad gave the beautiful flowers to Mom on their special day.

5. Wouldn't you say that horses are useful animals to own?

6. That Johnny is a willful boy; he is bent on having his own way.

7. I hope to win the cooking contest by baking my favorite chocolate chip cookies!

8. Is that a fistful of dried beans you are holding there?

9. This has been the most restful day I've had in months.

10. Kids, you need to be more thoughtful, and stop making so much noise while Dad naps.

11. Hey Mom, how thoughtful of you to make our favorite dinner tonight.

12. Eric, why don't you make yourself useful, and go get your work done?

13. Aunt April, when making the cookies, what will you use to sweeten them?

14. I am hopeful that when Sharon comes back from Kentucky, she will tell us stories of her travels.

15. I can hear that your metal pedal is squeaking a lot.

Lesson 54 ai

Vocabulary Words					Sight Words
bail	tail	train	wait	air	due
fail	gain	plain	waiter	fair	white
hail	main	chain	waist	hair	island
mail	pain	faint	daisy	pair	cause
nail	rain	paint	raisin	stair	buy
pail	stain	paid	aim	chair	leave
rail	brain	maid	claim	dairy	
sail	grain	maiden		fairy	

✱ The digraph 'ai' usually makes the "long a" vowel sound, like the name of the letter 'a'.

✱ Notice the silent 's' on the word "island."

✱ See Instructions Page 65.

Sentences

1. Hail has been pelting the roof for fifteen minutes or so.

2. Please do not fail to put a stamp on that and mail it.

3. Excuse me, Nick, help me reach the pail of nails so that I can finish nailing the grain bin together.

4. After we mend the rail, then let's paint it a plain white.

5. Ned, did you gain something from the lesson she gave?

6. Hey Mom, toss me the pail so I can bail out the boat!

7. Let's set sail for the main island because it's due to rain.

8. Jeff stepped on the cat's tail and it caused her great pain!

9. Hey Tom, you should get on that train before it leaves without you!

10. Oh dear, that sloppy waiter dropped the food all over Daisy and caused a big stain on her beautiful dress.

11. Our maid said she buys raisins at the store next door.

12. My aim is to wait until I get paid, then buy the pretty silver chain for the maiden that I love!

13. Is that a silk sash you have around your waist?

14. The train is carrying grain for the ranchers to buy.

15. That woman who worked at the fair has blond hair.

16. Uncle Ned bought Mom a pair of French chairs.

17. Grandfather used to live on a dairy farm when he was little, and he always got to drink fresh milk.

18. My little brother still believes in the tooth fairy.

Lesson 55   ay

Vocabulary Words					Sight Words
bay	Jay	pay	clay	tray	welcome
day	Kay	Ray	play	stay	table
Fay	lay	say	gray	stray	Susan
hay	may	way	pray	crayon	enough
					serve

✳ The letters 'ay' usually make the sound of the long (a).

✳ Notice the word "enough" in the sight words. The letters 'gh' sometimes sound like (f).

✳ See Instructions Page 65.

Sentences

1. Children have fun playing with clay and using crayons.

2. Let us pray that our mom will get better soon.

3. A stray dog has been hanging around outside our house again.

4. Grandfather thinks we paid way too much for the hay.

5. He said next time we shouldn't pay more than six dollars.

6. Let's watch Uncle Jim spray paint the gray trays a sparkling red.

7. Oh Uncle Robert, will you stay longer?

154

8. I can't wait until Uncle Jed's boat comes into the bay!

9. That stack of hay is enough to last the horses all winter.

10. Every night that gray dog bays at the moon for an hour.

11. What do you say, shall we go out to dinner tonight?

12. Susan, go ahead and welcome our friends to the table, and we will serve the meal right away.

13. When someone tells you "Thank you," it is good manners to say, "You're welcome."

14. Aunt Susan's pay was sent to her, and it was enough to pay all of her bills.

15. Dad, can Fred stay longer so that we can go outside and play ball?

Lesson 56   oa

Vocabulary Words					Sight Words
oat	load	soap	coach	oar	poor
boat	road	loaf	roach	boar	new
coat	toad	foam	boast	roar	bread
goat	Joan	coal	coast	board	lion
moat	loan	foal	roast	hoard	part
float	moan	goal	toast		course

✳ The letters 'oa' usually make the sound of the long (o).

✳ See Instructions Page 65.

Sentences

1. If you're going to roam around out there on a windy night, you'd better get your coat on!

2. I'm glad the goat has eaten all of her oats.

3. I am hungry too; let's go make us some toast with jelly.

4. The gust of wind is sending the ship up the coast.

5. Did you hear that the campers are roasting meat?

6. Look at that poor old horse pulling that great big load down the road all by himself.

7. Our goal is to get that load of coal to the train in time.

8. Eric's new coach is training the boys to be good football players. Of course, he tells the boys, "No pain, no gain!"

9. I love the part in the story where the fairy turns the pumpkin into a coach to be pulled by horses!

10. Oh dear, I saw some cockroaches in the kitchen!

11. My big brother moans about paying off his car loan.

12. Mom, I picked up a loaf of bread from the store for you.

13. Oh my goodness, did you hear that lion roar at the zoo?

14. Hey Joan, why don't we get out of the boat and float on our backs in the cool water?

15. Let's be sure to clean our hands really well with soap.

16. Grandpa said that if you lean a wooden board up against the back of the truck, it will make a ramp and will make loading easier.

Lesson 57   Sound of long o ow

Vocabulary Words					Sight Words
bow	blow	show	yellow	follow	high
mow	grow	slow	shadow	hollow	through
row	crow	snow	window		laugh
low	throw	fellow	shallow		birthday
					garden

✱ Here the letters 'ow' have the same sound as the name of the letter (o).

✱ Notice in "high" and "through" the 'gh' is silent. In "laugh", the 'gh' sounds like (f).

✱ See Instructions Page 65.

Sentences

1. Please show me how to tie a bow in my hair with these pretty yellow ribbons.

2. Someone needs to mow the grass; it has grown this high.

3. Do you think that grass can grow as high as a window?

4. The tall gray house is casting a shadow across the snow.

5. Slow the horse down quickly or she will run right through Mom's garden plants!

6. Are you men going to row the boat out to sea now?

7. On my birthday, I like blowing out the candles.

8. I am watching the crows fly low over the crops.

9. Did the children throw enough bread to the ducks?

10. They weren't throwing bread; they were throwing crackers to the ducks in the pond.

11. Did you fellows ever play in the snow when you were kids, like I did?

12. My brothers and I played in snow in back of our house when we lived back east.

13. My dad would laugh and remind us to not eat the snow if it was yellow.

14. Why are crops always planted in neat little rows?

15. Let's throw a great party for sister's birthday!

Lesson 58   ou

Vocabulary Words					Sight Words
thou	found	ground	south	our	commandment
loud	hound	out	douse	sour	fire
cloud	mound	pout	house	flour	false
proud	pound	about	mouse	scour	heard
ouch	round	trout	blouse	fountain	caught
bound	sound	mouth	lousy	thousand	

✻ The letters 'ou' are a diphthong, which is two letters put together which make a sliding sound. We have already seen the sound of 'ou' in the words "about" and "house."

✻ See Instructions Page 65.

Sentences

1. When my brother, Paul, went hunting this past summer, he found a poor lost hound dog, and took it home.

2. What was that loud sound we just heard?

3. One of the Ten Commandments is "Thou shall not bear false witness." That means don't lie.

4. There are gray clouds in the sky, and you can tell it's bound to rain sometime soon.

5. Dad is so proud of the twenty-pound trout he caught when he went fishing with the other fellows.

6. Miss Kitty asked a thousand times if we could go on a picnic.

7. We need to keep on traveling until we get to the fresh, beautiful fountain at the end of the road.

8. My poor dear, I saw you drop your cookie on the ground, but there's no need to pout about it. There are more.

9. Take that candy out of your mouth; you haven't had your dinner yet.

10. Susan is proud of her pretty green blouse.

11. Tell Miss Sweeney I need her to scour out those filthy pans right now.

12. Oh no, the gallon of milk you bought has gone sour.

13. That lousy mouse has gotten into my house again and has tracked flour all over the kitchen counter!

14. Quickly, douse the fire with the bucket of dish water!

15. Hey Mack, we heard that you caught a fantastic trout over there in the mountain stream!

Lesson 59 ow

Vocabulary Words				Sight Words	
bow	gown	tower	howl	farmer	remember
cow	town	flower	growl	prince	strength
how	brown	shower	towel	princess	handsome
now	clown	crowd		young	
sow	crown	powder		climb	
down	power	owl			

✳ In this lesson we have another diphthong, two letters put together to make a sliding sound. The sound of 'ow' in this lesson is the same as the 'ou' in the last lesson.

✳ See Instructions Page 65.

Sentences

1. Did you know that a mama pig is called a sow?

2. Farmer John, I see that you have bought yourself one fine, brown cow and a fat, pink sow.

3. Let's go downtown and buy Mother a new silk gown!

4. Now watch the silly clown take a bow since he is finished with his funny act.

5. That handsome, tall, young prince climbed many stairs up the tower to kiss the princess and give her a crown.

6. My dear sister, I wish you could have seen my handsome fellow shower me with flowers!

7. All of a sudden, snow started falling like white powder from the sky!

8. My silly hound dog growls at people who are my friends, and howls at the moon until midnight every Sunday!

9. I like to watch the owl blink his eyes up in the tree.

10. Turn on the power and let's crowd around the air cooler.

11. Dear, be sure to take a towel from the shelf before you start a shower. You don't want to drip water everywhere.

12. Those two fellows were laughing so hard, I would say they were howling with laughter!

13. Remember to put on some powder after your shower.

14. Let's quickly go downtown to see the prince and princess who have come to visit!

15. Does the farmer have enough strength to pull that sow out of the deep mud?

Lesson 60   aw au

Vocabulary Words					Sight Words
caw	draw	yawn	shawl	fault	picture
law	straw	drawn	awful	August	
saw	hawk	bawl	Paul	Austin	
claw	lawn	drawl	haul		

✳ The letters "aw" and "au" make the sound of (o) in "hot." We have seen this already in the words "saw" and "Paul."

✳ See Instructions Page 65.

Sentences

1. There is a law that says we shouldn't drive too fast on the road.

2. Sandy didn't see the cat's claws until the cat stuck out her paw and scratched her. Sandy bawled.

3. Paul always likes to drink his sun tea with a long straw.

4. Just a minute ago, I saw a hawk fly over our lawn.

5. I got to watch my Aunt Sharon draw a quick sketch of some beautiful flowers in the springtime.

6. Oh really? She has also drawn many lovely pictures of young children playing in the sprinkler.

7. I was saddened when the baby bawled for his mommy as he crawled away from me.

8. Aunt Vera thinks it is simply awful how hot it gets in our town in the month of August.

9. Whose fault is it that there is chocolate milk spilled on Mom's new white shawl?

10. I know Robert needs to get some sleep because he keeps yawning.

11. Stanford, please haul that load of hay to town today.

12. It's not my fault that it rained today and I couldn't mow the lawns.

13. Stop your bawling, it is your fault that you got a speeding ticket; you were going way too fast!

14. When I think of my brother, George, I start laughing.

15. His drawl makes me laugh so hard!

16. Sometimes I think it should be against the law to be so funny.

Lesson 61   oi oy

Vocabulary Words				Sight Words
oil	spoil	boy	Troy	refrigerator
boil	joint	coy	ahoy	temperature
coil	point	joy	poison	Fahrenheit
soil	foist	Roy		heart
toil	hoist	soy		oleander
broil	moist	toy		Mexico

✻ In this lesson, we learn another diphthong, where two letters are put together and they slide to make a new sound. The combinations 'oi' and 'oy' sound the same. We have heard this sound already in the word "boy."

✻ See Instructions Page 65.

Sentences

1. Boy! Did you see the oil spill all over the road after the truck crashed? The street was slick, slippery and moist.

2. Our sea captain, Roy, shouted, "Ahoy there!"

3. The small child was joyful after being given a new toy.

4. Don't let your horse eat leaves from the oleander bush, for it is poison to horses!

5. Grandma's joints hurt. She puts ointment on her joints, and the ointment smells like mint.

6. Of course, you know that the milk will spoil if it is left at room temperature for too long. Please put it back in the refrigerator.

7. Those poor boys have been toiling in the soil, planting seeds, all day long. Let's get them a cool drink of water.

8. Those pigs can talk! I heard them say "oink."

9. If you are at sea level, then to bring water to a boil, the water needs to be heated to 212 degrees Fahrenheit.

10. If you are boiling eggs, let them boil for about ten minutes.

11. Oh goody! Uncle Fred will be making dinner for us. I like the way Uncle Fred broils the chicken.

12. Troy made a point to say that the red heart was yours.

13. Uncle Don loves to sing, "I've got the joy, joy, joy, joy down in my heart!"

14. Dad asked us to try a drink of soy milk, and it was okay.

15. Sandy is being coy and does not want to ask Brent to come with her to the family picnic.

16. When my brother didn't want to do his work, he tried to foist it on me, but I said, "Do your own work, Bud!"

Lesson 62   __a, __ent

Vocabulary Words			Sight Words
Africa	Linda	resident	north
America	Pamela	different	live
Canada	Paula	instrument	ride
camera	president		place
			dessert
			Anne

✷ Here we have an 'a' or an 'ent' at the end of the word.

✷ Notice the word "dessert" in the sight words. The only spelling difference in dessert and desert is the added 's' in dessert. Dessert is yummy sweet food you eat after a meal. I remember to double the letter 's' by saying "Dessert is doubly delicious."

✷ See Instructions Page 65.

Sentences

1. My sister, Sharon, has asked me to go to Canada with her. Canada is in North America.

2. When my family gets together, my mother loves to take pictures with her little camera.

3. How many different classes will you be taking when you begin high school in the fall?

4. In America, we have a president to lead us, not a king.

5. When you live somewhere, you are called a resident of that place.

6. Maybe tomorrow we can try to cook a different kind of pie, rather than your favorite, pumpkin pie.

7. Uncle Bob loves to tell us of his many travels to the jungles of Africa.

8. Please think about running for president of our club. You would do a great job, Anne.

9. Are you a resident of Canada, America or Mexico?

10. I made a list of my favorite kinds of dessert: ice cream, apple cobbler, cherry pie, and chocolate cake.

11. Will you grab that camera, quickly, so that I can take a picture of the president as he passes this way?

12. How interesting, that actress has a different way of doing her hair and make-up!

13. Let me ride with you to pick up the desserts for the party.

14. Way up north it snows in the winter, and it is much colder than where we live.

Lesson 63   a__, be__

Vocabulary Words				Sight Words	
about	asleep	beside	below	Luke	key
afraid	begin	beyond	belief	Emily	monkey
agree	begun	betray		wise	grief
allow	before	believe		cousin	charm
				truth	daughter

✳ Sometimes 'a' or 'be' at the beginning of a word is a separate chunk, or syllable.

✳ See Instructions Page 65.

Sentences

1. Gus is afraid that Susan is about to get sick from eating too much candy, desserts and sweets.

2. Paula will agree to clean all of the dishes if Linda will begin to mop and sweep the floors. Do you think they can come to an agreement?

3. Believe me when I say that Dad and I will never allow you to go to the movies with Aunt Patty again!

4. Shh, shh! Little Luke has begun to fall asleep while sitting there between his brothers.

5. Woops, I'm sorry, but I seemed to have dropped my keys and they have fallen below your car seat.

6. Wow! Luke really seems to be taken with your daughter's charm and beauty.

7. The truth is, cousin Anthony is having problems spending his money wisely.

8. Please do not betray my trust in you.

9. If you will drive just beyond that hill, we will see a waterfall that is so lovely, it is beyond belief.

10. Emily is my daughter and Luke is her friend.

11. The man's sons and daughters are very sad that he passed away; they have much grief.

12. Glen left the picnic basket below the tree.

13. Is that a monkey I see in the tree? I didn't think they lived around here. I thought they were just in zoos.

14. Annie gave Emily a key to our house because she might get here before we come back.

15. Patrick has begun to understand what you mean.

Lesson 64   e__, de__

Vocabulary Words				Sight Words
electric	decoy	deliver	destroy	worry
eleven	defend	demand	develop	company
eleventh	defense	derail	development	banquet
debunk	defeat	detail		hurry
				bush
				harsh

✳ Sometimes the letters 'e' or 'de' at the beginning of a word is a separate chunk, or syllable.

✳ See Instructions Page 65.

Sentences

1. Don't worry, our company will try to deliver your goods to you by train within eleven days.

2. The mean king told his poor subjects, "I demand that you work for me every day, even if you do not want to!"

3. If we don't hurry and do something drastic, I'm afraid the bugs will destroy our crops very quickly.

4. Did Austin's team from Canada defeat the team from America? They are both great teams!

5. Will the Army defend their people so they can keep their freedom?

6. When Dad goes duck hunting, he often uses a decoy to fool the ducks into coming out of the bushes.

7. Is your new lamp an electric or gas lamp?

8. At the eleventh hour the bell rang eleven times.

9. In the event that I win one million dollars, I will give some money to everyone in my family!

10. Even if you can get a fire going, I don't think this old stone house will ever warm up!

11. You did a great job of finishing up every last detail of the paint job on that old big house.

12. At the company banquet, did they serve dessert after the main course was eaten?

13. I have been worrying that our team will be defeated by the new team in town, which everyone is talking about.

14. Mom says that we should not worry about it, but just do our best.

15. I demand that you get over here and clean up your mess!

Lesson 65   re__, pre__, in__

Vocabulary Words				Sight Words
recheck	resent	prefer	infect	shake
rebound	result	present	insect	listen
remember	redo	pretend	inside	write
repeat	return	prevent	invest	Tyler
report	revisit	indoors	innermost	guy

* Sometimes 're,' 'pre,' or 'in' at the beginning of a word is a separate chunk, or syllable.

* Some of these beginning syllables are prefixes. Prefixes are added to a root word to add to or change the meaning such as the following: 're' means "to do it again"; 'pre' means "before"; 'in' means "inside."

* See Instructions Page 65.

Sentences

1. Hey, let's pretend that we are firefighters and are going indoors to put out a kitchen fire!

2. Tyler would now like to present to you his report about insects.

3. Greg remembered it's Alice's birthday, and he has a present for her. He prefers to give it to her at her party later.

4. Sometimes special friends tell their innermost feelings.

5. "If you want to prevent a big spill, you had better watch where you lay that big glass down," said Sally.

6. Jack said, "I don't like to repeat myself, but please remember to put the trash out tonight, Tyler!"

7. Listen to that guy; he is repeating himself over and over.

8. Frank said, "I will admit that I resent my old teacher for hurting my feelings last year. I should forgive her for being mean that one time."

9. After we watched the movie in class yesterday, we had to write a detailed report about it for homework.

10. What are the results of the test you took last week, Robert?

11. Clint said, "I have checked and rechecked my report, and I think I am ready to turn it in tomorrow."

12. Since the new dress does not fit Lee well, she is planning to return it to the store pretty soon.

13. That basketball player, Dean, is so tall; he is good at getting rebounds.

14. Jean is afraid that our house is infested with insects!

15. Since it is so hot and muggy outdoors, let's stay indoors, Gail.

Lesson 66   Silent e (a_e)

Vocabulary Words				Sight Words	
ate	bake	came	parade	care	bye
date	cake	name	lemonade	dare	wild
gate	lake	same	cape	fare	child
hate	make	blame	grape	hare	honey
late	take	flame	shape	mare	sold
skate	flake	became	scrape	share	carrots
plate	shake	made	escape	spare	explore
cave	snake	blade	ape	square	sweetheart
save	awake	grade	chase	stare	
wave	mistake	shade	taste		

* This is an extremely important rule: the "silent e" rule. When a word ends with the following pattern: one vowel, one consonant, then an 'e,' then the single vowel says its name, and the final 'e' is absolutely silent. For example, see what happens when a "silent e" is added to these words: "at" becomes "ate"; "hat" becomes "hate"; "Sam" becomes "same"; "car" becomes "care"; "far" becomes "fare."

* When a vowel sounds like the name of its letter, we call that a long sound. Therefore, "same" has a long 'a' sound and "Sam" has a short 'a' sound.

* See Instructions Page 65.

Sentences

1. Zack says, "I hate to be late when we go to the movies."

2. "Yes, Mom, I ate all of the carrots on my plate," said Robin.

3. Let's wave good-bye, then go explore the cave!

4. They forgave Ray after he made that mistake in the game.

5. Sweetheart, let's bake a chocolate cake and take it to the second grade classroom for our son's class party.

6. Chad wants to go see the parade and taste the fresh-squeezed lemonade which will be sold in the nearby stands.

7. Can your child tell what shape a grape is?

8. Your crayon is a lovely shade of pink, I'll trade you.

9. Let's chase that man and grab his black cape.

10. Wow! There are snowflakes falling from the sky!

11. That poor ape fell from the tree and scraped his elbow; I saw it happen!

12. Brittney became angry when Mr. Weaver blamed her again for stepping on his flower garden.

13. Emily has been taught that you should shake someone's hand when meeting them for the first time.

14. The flames from the fire were shooting into the sky.

15. The man used a cane to help him walk from here to there.

16. Mom, do you care if I give my share of cookies to Gus?

17. A wild rabbit is called a hare.

18. If someone says "I dare you," you can say, "No thank you, I don't play that game."

Lesson 67   Silent e (i_e)

Vocabulary Words					Sight Words
dine	dime	hide	bite	file	assistant
fine	time	ride	kite	mile	native
line	five	side	quite	pile	fugitive
mine	hive	slide	white	smile	promise
nine	drive	beside	invite	awhile	opposite
vine	alive	inside	polite	tire	Gomez
shine	arrive	divide	bike	hire	Logan

✱ As we learned in lesson 66, when there is an 'e' at the end of a word, and it follows a single vowel and consonant, then the vowel says its name, and the final 'e' is absolutely silent. For example, notice what happens when "silent e" is added to these words: "fin" becomes "fine"; "shin" becomes "shine"; "dim" becomes "dime"; "Tim" becomes "time"; "hid" becomes "hide." "Tim" has a short 'i' sound, and "time" has a long 'i' sound.

✱ In the sight words, we have included some irregular words that do not follow the "silent e" rule. Each of the words in the sight words list keep the short 'i' sound.

✱ See Instructions Page 65.

Sentences

1. This is a fine time to take a five-mile hike or ride a bike.

2. Clementine loves to see Aunt Betty smile when Uncle Ray invites her out on a date.

3. Mrs. Cook said she would like to live beside a lake for awhile when she retires.

4. Dad, please give me that kite so I can hook a white tail to it.

5. Tammy wishes you would forgive her for not keeping her promise to arrive on time for the show.

6. I read that this flower is native to this part of the state.

7. Dean is not quite ready to hunt for treasure because he is still on the opposite side of the lake.

8. Ms. Gomez is very busy. She has quite a lot of papers in a pile for her assistant to file.

9. It will be good to get inside the cabin, slide into a warm bed, and thaw out from this freezing cold air.

10. Please hand me that silver fishing line; it is mine.

11. Don't get near that bee hive, or you might get stung!

12. That guy was not polite; he was quite the opposite.

13. As I was riding my new bike, Logan's dog tried to bite me!

14. If you take Danny for a drive, he promises to not bug you.

15. It's cool how that vine is climbing up the wall as it grows.

16. Logan is a fugitive from the law, and they haven't found him yet.

Lesson 68   Silent e (o_e)

Vocabulary Words					Sight Words
joke	hone	hose	stole	sore	wrote
woke	lone	rose	note	tore	Thanksgiving
broke	alone	chose	vote	shore	Christmas
smoke	shone	close	home	snore	December
spoke	stone	those	hope	store	November
awoke	throne	suppose	rope	before	Tuesday
bone	code	hole	bore		Sylvia
cone	dose	pole	more		England
					morning
					Jose

✳ As we learned in lessons 66 and 67, when there is an 'e' at the end of a word, and it follows a single vowel and consonant, then the vowel says its name, and the final 'e' is absolutely silent. For example, "bon" becomes "bone"; "con" becomes "cone"; "not" becomes "note"; "hop" becomes "hope."

✳ See Instructions Page 65.

Sentences

1. This is no joke; I woke up and smelled smoke coming from the stove in our home this morning!

2. If you put your nose any closer to that rose, that bee might sting you.

3. The Queen of England sat on her throne in front of the people.

4. My misbehaving little brothers broke all seven windows by throwing stones at them!

5. Those students are supposed to take the test alone, but they chose to get together and cheat.

6. The water hose broke on my mom's old, battered car. Mom is very upset about it.

7. The moon shone through the clouds late that night.

8. When Aunt Sylvia awoke, her son, Jose, was eating an ice cream cone and had made a mess all over the kitchen.

9. Ouch! I believe I broke the tiny bones in my hand!

10. Those people need to dig a hole so they can put the pole into it.

11. Why don't you close that door; it's getting cold in here.

12. Kay, be sure to vote next Tuesday before you get home.

13. Hank wrote himself a note to help him remember.

14. When my son and daughter come for Thanksgiving in November, I hope they stay for three weeks.

15. Next December, all of our close family members will gather at Grandma and Grandpa's home for Christmas.

16. Hey Dad, are you sore from riding the horse all day?

Lesson 69   Silent e (u_e) & (e_e)

Vocabulary Words				**Sight Words**
dude	tune	cube	Pete	excited
crude	prune	tube	complete	find
include	rule	cure	concrete	lady
nude	use	pure	Eve	party
dune	excuse	figure	Steve	piano
June	brute	cute	these	learn
		compute		Joe

✳ As we learned in lessons 66 and 67, when there is an 'e' at the end of a word, and it follows a single vowel and consonant, then the vowel says its name, and the final 'e' is absolutely silent. For example, "dud" becomes "dude"; "crud" becomes "crude"; "us" becomes "use"; "cub" becomes "cube"; "cut" becomes "cute"; "pet" becomes "Pete."

✳ See Instructions Page 65.

Sentences

1. Hey guys, did Pete and Steve ever complete the tile job they began last June?

2. These concrete sidewalks were laid many years ago.

3. On Christmas Eve our children get so excited about opening their presents.

4. Please excuse me, but may I use your watch for a minute?

5. We will need a lot of ice cubes, so include that on your shopping list for the party.

6. Those boys are being so crude right next to that lady!

7. Oh, listen to that lovely tune he is playing on the piano!

8. Did the class learn the rules or were the students still confused when class was over?

9. Those cute children love to slide down the waterslide on the big black inner tube.

10. When I grow up I want to play a flute like my Uncle Joe.

11. Sometimes Mom makes me eat prunes because she says they are supposed to be good for me.

12. Hey dude, are you going to get out of my way or not?

13. When a person does not have any clothes on, then that person is nude.

14. My friend has an illness, and I hope someone will figure out the cure soon.

15. My bracelet is pure silver.

16. That boy is a brute! I told my friend, Eve, that it does not matter if he is cute!

Lesson 70   or

Vocabulary Words					Sight Words
or	cork	sort	corn	porch	Nancy
for	fork	short	horn	torch	Janice
Ford	form	snort	torn	scorch	Sherry
Lord	orbit	sport	scorn	normal	Chris
nor	order	corner	thorn	organ	comfort
snore	fort	born	morning	Oregon	paper
					Ramirez
					brought

✱ In this lesson, the letter combination 'or' makes the sound as in the word "for."

✱ See Instructions Page 65.

Sentences

1. Hey Nancy, is that car you just bought a Ford?

2. Let's go sit on the porch and swing for awhile.

3. Joan brought a torch to the beach party. She didn't need to because there is enough moonlight!

4. It was funny to watch Janice pull the cork out of the bottle, because she fell down while doing it.

5. Are these hot dogs made from pork, chicken or beef?

6. Last summer our family went to New York to see our friends, Sherry and Chris.

7. I love to see those kids laughing in the fort that Dad put together last spring.

8. You had better watch out for thorns in those roses!

9. In this sport, it is not normal to see short players.

10. There is a news report about the storm in the south.

11. My big sisters live in the dorm at school.

12. Farmer Morton is growing corn on his farm.

13. Joan's horse snorted when it was offered an apple.

14. We will need to abort that plan to make a tent because the cloth is torn and scorched.

15. I am sure that Jake was born in Oregon blowing his horn.

16. Jake looks silly the way he uses his fork.

17. We do not need to sort nor stack these sheets of paper.

18. Listening to her sing and play the organ every morning is a comfort to my ears.

185

Lesson 71   ar

Vocabulary Words					Sight Words
bar	smart	hard	barn	barber	music
car	chart	yard	farm	garden	wear
far	harp	ark	harm	pardon	open
jar	sharp	lark	part	March	Noah
star	scarf	mark	apart	market	George
start	card	park	alarm	marble	
				farther	

✳ The letters 'ar' make the sound as in the word "car."

✳ See Instructions Page 65.

Sentences

1. I tried to open the jar, but it is too hard for me.

2. On Grandpa's farm, there are cats hiding in the barn.

3. Steve and Chris like to take toys apart out in the yard.

4. Did that sharp blade cause any harm to Sherry?

5. Pete and George are playing with marbles in the garden.

6. The alarm sounded when Carmen bumped her car.

7. It brings joy to my heart to listen to Mrs. Ramirez play the harp.

8. In March, the wind kicks up and I have to wear a scarf around my neck when we ride to the market.

9. Please mark your paper at the top, on the far right side.

10. It is time to go to the barber to get your hair cut.

11. Farther along in the play, there will be an exciting part.

12. You are smart, and you know the names of the planets.

13. Please hand me those white charts on the table.

14. Todd needs to finish working in the yard and the garden.

15. Let's go to the park, have a picnic, and watch the larks fly over us in the sky.

16. Have you heard the story of Noah and the Ark?

17. Pardon me, George, but will you take this alarm apart for me and figure out what the problem is?

Lesson 72   er

Vocabulary Words					Sight Words
her	perfect	serve	dessert	operate	wash
fern	perhaps	servant	desert	federal	reduce
clerk	person	deserve	verse	battery	garage
jerk	stern	swerve	bakery		delicious
					violin

✳ The letters 'er' make the sound as in the word "her."

✳ See Instructions Page 65.

Sentences

1. Don't jerk the ladder; hold it still for me, please!

2. Did you tell the clerk about the spill on the floor?

3. Beautiful green ferns are growing in my garden.

4. I had to swerve in order to miss that truck!

5. You are such a good person; you deserve to sit back and let me serve you some delicious dessert.

6. A servant is someone who serves another person.

7. We should each wash our hands often to help us not get sick.

8. Mrs. Fox, can we put a new battery in that music player so it will operate?

9. Those guys had a lot of nerve stealing my new lavender car right out of my garage!

10. It seems that the new clerk you hired to work the night shift is working out perfectly, right?

11. I'd rather be sweet and kind to children, but sometimes I have to be stern with them to get them to behave.

12. Can ferns grow in the mountains or in the desert?

13. If I were deserted on an island, I would want to be with my best friends, Robert and Herman.

14. I really want to live in Washington because I love the rain.

15. Perhaps when I grow up I will learn to play the violin and piano, because they make beautiful music.

16. I would love for her to play all of the verses of my favorite song!

Lesson 73   ir

Vocabulary Words				Sight Words
sir	dirt	girdle	firm	Carol
fir	dirty	girth	affirm	Carolyn
stir	shirt	mirth	confirm	April
whir	skirt	birth	thirty	autumn
first	girl	birthday	thirteen	California
thirst	bird	shirk	stirrup	
thirsty	third	quirk		

＊ The letters 'ir' make the same sound we hear in the word "first."

＊ See Instructions Page 65.

Sentences

1. The first lady I saw said, "Good day, sir, may I help you?"

2. Excuse me, sir, but there is some dirt on your shirt.

3. On the third of September, before autumn begins, I plan to travel to Mexico to visit my sister, Carolyn.

4. There are thirty birds for sale in that pet store.

5. I can confirm that I have been wearing a girdle for thirteen years!

6. Did you get a new skirt for your birthday?

7. Carol enjoys watching the fir tree stir in the wind.

8. A quirky thing happens when I look at Paul; my eye twitches!

9. My daughters, April and Carolyn, are traveling to California in the autumn of this year.

10. You have work to do; don't shirk it off!

11. Ask Katie to help you clean the dirt off your skirt, Carol.

12. Please inform Janice that her bird won't stop squawking; I can't sleep!

13. The boys are thrilled that the girls have been invited over for a birthday party for the third time this month.

14. When you ride a horse, you sit on the saddle and put your feet in the stirrups.

15. We call it "mirth" when there is happiness and joy.

16. Fay, should I stir the pan of chocolate milk on the stove?

17. Cass and Logan affirm your plan to clean out Grandpa's garage and get rid of all the piles and stacks of old papers.

Lesson 74   ur

Vocabulary Words					Sight Words
fur	hurl	spurn	curse	Saturday	Michael
slur	burn	curt	nurse	church	usually
spur	turn	hurt	purse	purple	heavily
curl	return	blurt	curve	murmur	word
furl	churn	spurt	Thursday		color
					Jasmine

✳ The letters 'ur' make the same sound we hear in the word "fur."

✳ See Instructions Page 65.

Sentences

1. Feel the soft fur of the kitty when he curls up on your lap.

2. Jasmine, you should return to the kitchen to check on the food that you are cooking before it burns.

3. Does it usually hurt when the nurse gives you a shot?

4. I could tell that Miss Clementine was angry when we spoke last April because her words were curt and she would not smile.

5. Purple is Katie's favorite color, and she wears it often.

6. Stop your cursing right now! Choose better words.

7. Jordan goes to church on Saturdays; Nancy goes on Sundays.

8. Be careful, Becky, there is a curve in the road ahead.

9. Mrs. Gray blurted her answer out so fast, Mr. Taft jerked!

10. The soft, white snow was falling heavily all around us.

11. Speak slowly and do not slur your words together.

12. Michael, please turn off the stove before you leave the kitchen.

13. Oh dear, Sylvia left her purse in the shopping cart today.

14. Have you ever churned the cream to make butter?

15. Unfurl the flag so we can get a good look at it.

16. Water spurts out of the hose when you hold it like that.

17. Usually Austin spurs Jeff to work his hardest because he sets a good example.

18. Emily wouldn't stop murmuring, so in the end Robert blurted out, "I've had enough, just stop!"

Lesson 75   Sound of (er) or ar

Vocabulary Words			Sight Words
color	history	separate	group
word	regular	forward	salad
work	orchard	backward	sentences
worm	calendar	upward	Mackenzie
world	caterpillar	downward	Juanita
worse	vinegar	afterward	Kylie
worth	particular		toward

✴ The words in this lesson have letter combinations 'or' or 'ar' with the unusual sound of 'er' that we hear in "her."

✴ See Instructions Page 65.

Sentences

1. Allen Gomez can read each word in those sentences.

2. We have a lot of work to do, so let's get going!

3. Can Troy tell that the worms have been eating the plants?

4. That group of people has been traveling the world for more than twelve months!

5. If you do something wrong, then admit it. It is much worse to lie about it.

6. Can Huck tell me how much that warm coat is worth?

7. We are going to eat our lunch; then afterward we'll relax.

8. Will everyone move forward so that more friends can join us?

9. Farmer Dean regularly walks through his apple orchard.

10. Mr. Taft needs to check his calendar before agreeing to go to that meeting with his wife, Juanita.

11. Little Mackenzie enjoys watching caterpillars crawl on her hand.

12. Uncle Steve puts vinegar and oil in his salads.

13. Kylie forgot her coat at home. Is it worth going back to get it?

14. Ross regularly makes mistakes when taking history tests.

15. Be careful not to drive backwards instead of forwards.

16. Should Nancy adjust the rope upward or downward?

17. Parker says we should all work toward making the world a better place to live in.

18. Juanita got the word out to her friends that they could join her and her family for dinner.

Lesson 76

Sound of (or) — oor our ar oar

Vocabulary Words					**Sight Words**
door	pour	roar	hoarse	dwarf	Jared
floor	court	board	war	quart	Judy
moor	oar	hoard	warm	quarter	Judith
four	boar	coarse	warn	quarrel	cents
					Ethan

✳ These letter combinations all sound like (or) here. It is normal for 'oor' and 'oar' to sound like (or), but it is unusual for 'ar' and 'our' to sound like (or).

✳ See Instructions Page 65.

Sentences

1. Is little Jared three or four years old now?

2. Did Sherry tell Judy to pour the milk into the bowl?

3. Judith has to go to court because yesterday she got a ticket for speeding down the road.

4. Tell Noah to close the door because leaves are blowing into the room and onto the floor.

5. My older brother went away to fight in the war.

6. I am glad the campfire will keep us warm.

7. Ethan warned him not to go into that dark cave alone!

8. A dwarf is a person who does not grow to the normal size.

9. Judy is thirsty enough to drink one quart of water.

10. A quarter is a coin that is worth twenty-five cents.

11. I told Josh and Gus to stop quarreling, but they haven't.

12. Robert is hoarse because he has been yelling all morning at the football game!

13. Betty won't sit on that board because it is too coarse.

14. It is interesting how an animal will hoard food in its den.

15. A wild boar is related to a pig. I wouldn't want to be near one without a gate or wall between us because a wild boar can hurt people.

16. Chet told us about the roaring lion he saw at the zoo.

17. Chip and Zack enjoy rowing their boat with long oars.

18. My dad used to tell us how they would moor the ship so that it would not drift away.

19. Hey Justin, remember that one quarter of that money is mine.

Lesson 77

Sound of (air) —
ear eir arr ar uar

Vocabulary Words				Sight Words
bear	narrow	Mary	aquarium	broad
pear	sparrow	February	guarantee	gone
tear	carry	January	their	shoulder
wear	Harry	library	heir	second
arrow	marry	parent		

✳ These letter combinations all sound like (air). 'ear' usually sounds like (eer), but here they sound like (air).

✳ The word "heir" has a silent "h". Heir sounds like air.

✳ See Instructions Page 65.

Sentences

1. That big brown bear has a broad shoulder span.

2. The hungry children picked the pears off the pear tree, and now the tree is bare.

3. Did Harry really tear that new shirt he bought?

4. Chad likes to wear the shirt with a black arrow on it.

5. At this same hour every day, Cliff and Stan come running in to ask for their lunch.

6. Be careful on that narrow path. You could slip and fall.

7. That tiny brown bird in the window is called a sparrow.

8. January is the first month on the calendar and February is the second month.

9. Kip and Juanita love going to the library to get books.

10. Dan's child, Fay, is playing in the playground with Pam.

11. Harry saved up his money, then he bought an aquarium.

12. The hunter shot the bear with a bow and arrow.

13. Beth's parents own a dairy farm and have many brown dairy cows.

14. Where I live, I think February is the coldest month of winter.

15. Here, carry this backpack over your shoulders, please.

16. Lee and Bobby say that their parents are not home.

17. I cannot bear to see the hunters shoot the animals with guns or bows and arrows!

18. Hey Clint, can you carry this load of books to the library?

19. Tom and Frank have an aquarium full of colorful fish.

20. I guarantee you, Frank will marry his sweetheart, Judy, next autumn in a garden wedding.

Lesson 78

Sound of (e) — ea ai ie u ue

Vocabulary Words				Sight Words
dead	ready	meant	against	else
head	feather	heavy	friend	sense
read	leather	sweater	bury	salt
bread	weather	breakfast	guess	Jacob
spread	instead	again	guest	Jerry
				bacon
				Natha

These letter combinations make the sound of (e) as in "red."

✳ See Instructions Page 65.

Sentences

1. Jacob's friend came over to the house again and read to Jacob while he was sick and laying on the couch.

2. While Grandma was making bread, she forgot to put the salt in, so it didn't taste quite right.

3. Alex was sad when he went to bury his dead, pet rabbit.

4. Jerry, you know that it is against the rules to do that!

5. When the weather is snowing, Jacob puts a hat on his head.

6. I guess Mom was right when she said, "Nathan has a lot of common sense."

7. Thirty guests arrived here on time and we were ready!

8. When Jerry was helping his dad, he asked, "Is there anything else I can do for you, Dad?"

9. Allen uses a feather duster when he is asked to dust the benches in the North Chapel.

10. Mom, for breakfast can we have pancakes instead of bacon and eggs?

11. Sally loves the new sweater Aunt Jane gave her for Christmas!

12. It surprises me how a stack of paper can be so heavy!

13. I am sorry, Alex, I meant to tell you I wouldn't be coming.

14. The class made beautiful ornaments with feathers attached.

15. Alice says we need to shorten our list of guests to twelve.

16. Uncle Jay happens to be buried in work this week.

17. My friends sense that there's something wrong with me.

18. My head has been hurting for an hour because of the noise.

19. Leather purses, belts and wallets are made from the hides of animals.

Lesson 79   Sound of (oo) u o

Vocabulary Words			Sight Words
bush	bull	pudding	fence
push	full	during	bright
cushion	pull	wolf	probably
butcher	bulletin	woman	vacation

✳ In this lesson, the letters 'o' and 'u' make the sound of (oo) as in "book."

✳ See Instructions Page 65.

Sentences

1. Mrs. Green plans to plant a row of oleander bushes alongside this fence to help block the wind.

2. Children, do not push each other! Someone may get hurt.

3. Oh, your new couch has soft, plush cushions. I'm not getting up.

4. Next time don't fill your bowl so full of milk, it might spill again.

5. If the sun is too bright for your eyes, pull the shades down.

6. Stanley read this morning's bulletin to the entire group.

7. Vanilla pudding is a dessert that is very easy to make.

8. My husband is a butcher. He works at the market down the street.

9. During recess you should go to the bathroom and wash your hands with soap.

10. The campers saw a wolf up the mountain between some bushes and trees.

11. An adult girl is called a woman. If there is more than one adult girl, then together they are called women.

12. During my summer vacation, I traveled to many islands off the Atlantic coast of North America.

13. If you make that bull mad, he will probably run after you and try to gore you.

14. The woman who lives next door tells me that she often listens to soft music when she is resting.

15. On airplanes, the seat cushions can be used for floating in water.

16. Sometimes I need to push my son, Dan, to get him to complete his chores. But he is always eager to eat.

17. When Bud crashed his bike in the rose bushes, he probably got thorns in his britches.

Lesson 80

Sound of (oo) — ue ew ui oe o_e

Vocabulary Words			Sight Words
blue	new	move	Indian
clue	blew	remove	large
glue	chew	lose	student
true	drew	suit	lace
cruel	flew	fruit	vegetable
value	grew	shoe	few
Tuesday	screw	canoe	mew
	threw		view
			Elijah
			Mia

✳ These letter combinations make the sound of (oo) as in "moon."

✳ In the sight words, the letters 'ew' in few and mew and the letters 'iew' in view all sound like the word "you."

✳ See Instructions Page 65.

Sentences

1. The color blue is my favorite color in the world.

2. Why don't you try using glue to fix that broken toy?

3. Is it really true that the ugly monster is dead?

4. The way I view it, when a person is extremely mean and hurtful, we say he or she is cruel.

5. Next Tuesday, Sally has an appointment with her lawyer.

6. When Jared gets all dressed up, he wears his dark blue suit with a white shirt and neck tie.

7. Kids need to know that it is important to eat fruits and vegetables every day.

8. Eric, don't move your friend until someone checks to see if his foot is broken.

9. Sherry, go ahead and remove his shoe so we can see his foot.

10. Joe wrote a book about Native Americans, who are sometimes called American Indians.

11. When I was a student, I learned that a canoe is a long narrow boat made out of a hollow tree trunk.

12. Your shoe laces are loose, so you'd better tie them again.

13. Elijah, what answer did you choose for number fifteen on that hard English test that we took this morning?

14. Aunt Mia blew the candles out with one blow.

15. We are missing a few screws for that shelf.

Lesson 81

Sound of (ee) – ine, ile, ey, ie, ei
Sound of (i) – u, ui, ine

Vocabulary Words				Sight Words
figurine	key	chief	business	police
magazine	money	thief	build	concern
submarine	monkey	brief	built	none
sardine	honey	field	guitar	machine
gasoline	either	believe	Jasmine	Ryan
automobile	seize	busy	determine	
			engine	

✴ The first group of letter combinations make a sound like (ee) as in "keep." For example: "figurine," "automobile," "key," "chief," and "believe."

✴ The second group of letter combinations make a sound like (i) in "sit." For example: "busy," "build," and "Jasmine."

✴ See Instructions Page 65.

Sentences

1. The Native American chief is the one with all the feathers on his headdress.

2. The thief stole the money and buried it in the field.

3. After the thief was caught, the police seized the money.

4. I believe that my favorite fish is the tiny sardine.

5. The next automobile I buy will either be a Honda or a Ford.

6. The cost of gasoline is very high at the pump.

7. Madison enjoys watching monkeys at the zoo.

8. The engine in Chad's car stopped for a brief time.

9. Will either Dad or Uncle Joe remove the dead animal in the street?

10. We have been busy following the movements of the enemy's submarine.

11. Jack said to Ryan, "It's none of your business how I spend my money!"

12. Uncle Jacob built a business repairing copy machines.

13. Dad plans to build a house with the help of his brothers.

14. Did you see the jade figurine that Clint bought for Jasmine?

15. Brandon was wearing a leather jacket last night.

16. Honey, please determine your main concern so that we can discuss it together.

17. Did Alex understand the key point in the magazine story about guitars?

Lesson 82   Sound of (u) o ou oo o_e

Vocabulary Words					Sight Words
son	among	double	country	love	Sheryl
won	color	trouble	southern	dove	actually
month	cover	touch	blood	glove	recent
money	company	young	flood	above	search
Monday	nothing	cousin			error

✳ These letter combinations make an unusual sound here; they sound like (u) as in "cut".

✳ See Instructions Page 65.

Sentences

1. George actually won some money at the recent bingo game held at the lodge!

2. Son, I am proud of you for working hard this past month. Your paycheck will be bigger this month because you worked so hard.

3. Among other things, on Monday, Sheryl has to go over the company accounts to check for errors.

4. Gus said that Lee and Rick have done nothing about the mess they made at the party at his house.

5. Since the flowers have bloomed, the field is covered in a sea of beautiful colors of lavender, red, blue, yellow and pink.

6. Cousin Anna loves it when the doves perch in her fruit trees and coo in the late afternoon.

7. You will be happy to know that Karen found your brown leather gloves above the fireplace.

8. There is a major flood in the midwest part of our country, due to all the recent rains we have been having.

9. Mr. Tomkins knew his young, athletic daughter was in trouble when he saw the blood on her arm.

10. It's so sweet to watch the young baby boy reach up to touch his dad.

11. Last month each fifth grade student chose a country or state to research and write about.

12. Mike, please stand in front of the class and share your report on the country that you chose.

13. After the children color their pictures, they will print words at the top of each page to describe the picture.

14. Mom likes to tease and say those twins are double-trouble.

15. Judith's cousin is from the southern part of Africa.

16. Why does Mr. Johnson believe our country is in trouble?

Lesson 83   Long a

Vocabulary Words				Sight Words	
hazy	baby	able	David	alligator	sophomore
lazy	lady	table	Hazel	radiator	junior
crazy	bacon	stable	aviator	major	senior
Navy	apron	cradle	basis	radar	Carlos
				stadium	Santiago

✳ In this lesson, the letter 'a' sounds like the name of the letter 'a.'

✳ See Instructions Page 65.

Sentences

1. If you do not do your work, someone may call you "lazy!"

2. It's simply crazy to leave a baby on a table all alone. He could fall off and get hurt.

3. Aunt Hazel is cooking bacon and wearing an apron.

4. The Jones family was not able to come to the stables today to ride their horses.

5. I am truly afraid that there is an alligator in our back pond; don't anyone go back there!

6. I have heard that you are training to become an aviator so that you can fly your own plane. Is that true?

7. Our car's radiator is overheating. Let's allow the car to cool down; then we can add some cool water.

8. Sh! Sh! The baby is sleeping in the cradle and we don't want her to wake up for awhile!

9. Until David passes the test, he will not be able to drive a car by himself.

10. Mom thinks it is crazy for Uncle Carlos to join the Navy while our country is at war, but Dad says Uncle Carlos is brave.

11. Nancy, sit down at the table with me and let's talk about this.

12. Jessica is a freshman, a ninth grader, at Lakeside High School, in Lake Elsinore, California.

13. Jackie is a sophomore, a tenth grader, at El Capitan High School, in Lakeside, California

14. Ernest is a junior, an eleventh grader, at Mountain View High School, in Mountain View, California.

15. Sandra is excited about being a senior, a twelfth grader, at Santiago High School, in Corona, California

16. Mrs. Jensen has an interest in becoming an aviator, too, just like the rest of her daring family.

Lesson 84   Long e

Vocabulary Words			Sight Words
even	event	meter	phone
Steven	Sweden	Peter	except
evening	zebra	Felix	exhibit
eternity	secret	evil	union
economy	tepee		triangle

✳ In this lesson, the letter 'e' sounds like the name of the letter 'e.'

✳ See Instructions Page 65.

Sentences

1. Steven is my best friend, and it was a fantastic event when we went swimming in the lake this past summer.

2. Even if you don't agree with me, I still think that movie is all about evil; I will not see it with you.

3. Someday Mr. Hunter wants to go to Sweden for a vacation, since his relatives are from there.

4. Sometime this evening, Aunt Lauren is expecting an important phone call about her new job possibility.

5. My daughters are all excited about keeping a secret from their brother about his upcoming birthday party.

6. A tepee is a home which some Native Americans have used, and it looks like a triangular tent.

7. Did Peter tell you that he has to travel up north to buy a new machine for his company?

8. A zebra is an interesting animal; it kind of looks like a horse with stripes.

9. Tomorrow our cousins from Sweden will be arriving by plane for a big family reunion.

10. Jerome and Clifton are usually the first ones in the group to volunteer to help get things done.

11. Can you tell me why Peter has a gray tennis shoe on his right foot and a white tennis shoe on his left foot?

12. I enjoyed all of the fair exhibits except for that one at the very end of the table. It has a display of dead bugs and insects!

13. Actually, I figure that we won't find all of the freshmen until we search the baseball fields in back of the school.

14. I think it's cruel how you caught that poor moose!

15. What in the world was Sheryl thinking when she parked her car without putting coins in the parking meter?

Lesson 85   Long i

Vocabulary Words					Sight Words
hi	blind	item	pilot	client	mice
bind	grind	idle	tidy	silent	Capitol
find	behind	isolate	tiger	Siberia	government
kind	child	climate	spider	lion	Morgan
mind	mild	riot	vibrate	dandelion	Dr.
	wild				

✻ In this lesson, the letter 'i' sounds like the name of the letter 'i.'

✻ See Instructions Page 65.

Sentences

1. Jared killed a large spider. Let's see if we can find the spider web behind the old woodshed.

2. That pilot, Mr. Morgan, took us for a wild ride on his plane.

3. What kind of bushes are growing behind your house?

4. I wonder how the three mice in the story became blind.

5. Morgan, would you mind watching my child for awhile?

6. The miller grinds the grain at the mill in order to make flour for our bread.

7. So far it's been a mild winter, and the bright, yellow dandelions are still blossoming in the fields.

8. The zookeeper likes to tidy up the tiger's cage when the wild tiger is not there.

9. Please don't go near that lion behind the bars. He is isolated because he is wild and crazy.

10. Mr. Cleveland won't be idle for long, he's just resting a bit.

11. Remember to start each sentence with a capital letter.

12. The building where the federal government works is called the Capitol. There is an item in the newspaper about it today.

13. Landon is really in a bind, because of all the lies he has told.

14. I think that Jerry should expect the union to disagree with his point of view about how many hours we work.

15. That kind lady has such a mild manner about her.

16. You chose the wrong vegetables to plant at this time of year.

17. Dr. Linzey wants us to isolate all of the clients who have this particular disease and keep them separate from the others.

Lesson 86 Long o

Vocabulary Words					Sight Words
old	told	most	Jonah	radio	Julie
bold	scold	post	hero	auto	station
cold	roll	poster	zero	hello	substance
fold	toll	open	potato	ago	Russia
gold	troll	only	tomato	Roman	region
sold	pony	over	Eskimo	romantic	
	both	Jonas	opinion	control	

✳ In this lesson, the letter 'o' sounds like the name of the letter 'o.'

✳ See Instructions Page 65.

Sentences

1. Julie told me that it's cold only in her classroom.

2. Nicole, are you willing to help me fold the towels?

3. My great grandmother sold most of her gold coins.

4. I think Dad is going to scold my older brother, Kevin, for riding the tiny pony.

5. That story Miss Daisy read to us a long time ago, about the troll underneath the bridge, was my favorite story.

6. The substance of this news story is that the new toll road is open now, so most lanes will have less autos on them.

7. Please roll up the new posters that advertise the radio station, and drive them over to Mr. Grant's building.

8. Some natives from the arctic and subarctic regions of Canada, Alaska, and Russia are called Eskimos.

9. Our family grows fresh tomatoes on vines in the garden.

10. Aunt Shay and Uncle Jonas are coming over for dinner.

11. Mom fixes baked potatoes with butter and sour cream.

12. I loved the romantic part of the movie where the shy lady looked into the eyes of the handsome man and whispered, "You are my hero."

13. The teacher said, "Please control your excitement!"

14. Grandma and Grandpa like to listen to old radio shows.

15. Ice houses, called "igloos," have been used by the Eskimos.

16. I visited Uncle John's ranch in Montana where he raises Shetland Ponies.

17. Mom always tells us to eat our vegetables. My favorite vegetables are spinach and cauliflower.

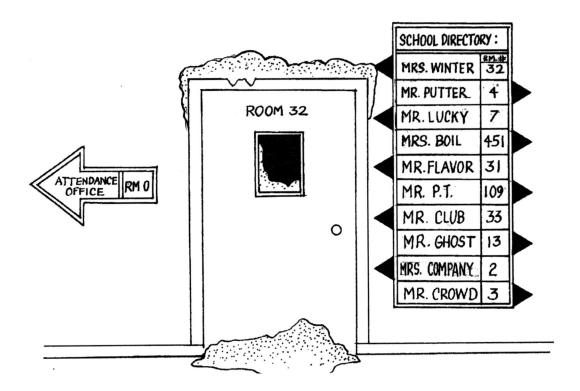

Lesson 87   Sound of long u — u ou

Vocabulary Words				Sight Words
music	cumulate	truth	ruin	calm
pupil	cumulative	bubonic	July	soldier
humidity	super	rhubarb	soup	famous
unique	tunic	student	group	theater
Uganda	tulip	curriculum	wound	plague

✳ In these words, the letters 'u' and 'ou' sound like the name of the letter 'u' or (oo) as in moon.

✳ See Instructions Page 65.

Sentences

1. Please turn on the soft music. It calms my nerves and helps me to relax.

2. To tell you the truth, I think these fifth grade pupils are the smartest students in the school!

3. Do not trample the tulip garden. You will ruin those beautiful flowers.

4. In July, a group of retired Army soldiers will get together to remember things that happened years ago and retell their stories of being in Europe during the bubonic plague.

5. Some of these retired soldiers were wounded during the war.

6. Some of them were shot, others were hurt from blasts, and others were wounded in different ways.

7. Uh oh, it smells like Granny is making her famous vegetable soup which none of us like.

8. Remember to be polite and thank Granny for the soup.

9. Mr. Hansen seems determined to develop his pupils into people who know and love classical music.

10. Have you ever eaten rhubarb pie? Aunt Hilda used to make it when I was a young child.

11. A large crowd is cumulating around the theater doors.

12. They are expecting a famous actress to come out any minute.

13. I was calm until you turned on your extremely unique, loud music! That ruined everything!

14. Hey Dad, this heat and humidity are unbearable, can we go to the theater to see a movie? It will surely be cooler in there.

15. Judy's shawl is very unique, did she bring it back with her from Uganda?

Lesson 88　　Soft c

Vocabulary Words　　　　　　　　　Sight Words

cent	process	mice	cancer	distance	stalk
center	December	nice	dance	difference	knocked
celery	decide	rice	chance	pencil	absolutely
cereal	bicycle	price	since	once	natural
certain	face	slice	Vince	piece	receive
circus	lace	twice	prince	practice	
cigar	race	advice	fence	surface	
city	place	ice	ounce	voice	
citizen	grace	icy	bounce	exercise	
accident	space	police	announce	decimal	
fancy	palace	sentence	balance	recent	

✻ In this lesson, we learn that the letter 'c' makes the sound of (s) when the letter 'e,' 'i' or 'y' comes after it. We call this a soft 'c' sound.

✻ See Instructions Page 65.

Sentences

1. Grandpa says that in the olden days it used to cost one cent to buy a stalk of celery at the farmer's market.

2. In the center of the table was a box of cereal, which little Jimmy accidentally knocked over and spilled everywhere.

3. I am absolutely certain that the Big Top Circus will be coming to our city next December, during our vacation!

4. Did that guy recently receive a cigar as a gift?

5. The people who are born in a certain country are called natural citizens of that country.

6. John can't decide whether or not to enter the bicycle race.

7. In the palace, the ladies wear lovely lace on their evening gowns, and they walk so gracefully.

8. There certainly is enough space available in this place to hold a dance for fifty people.

9. What do you think the chance is that Prince Charles will come and shake my hand at tomorrow's event?

10. Since the fence was built around the farm, there has been a difference in the number of animals that have escaped.

11. I want you to get a piece of paper and a pencil so that you can write down the sentences that I dictate to you.

12. I will tell you only once more to drink all of your juice!

13. Did you hear the announcement about the results of the long distance race? I hope my sister, Shirley, won.

14. Grandma almost lost her balance while climbing the stairs!

15. Twice, the police gave advice to stay off the slippery road. The surface was covered with ice.

16. The storm knocked out power for the second time this month. Twice now we've had to go through the process of repairing the electrical lines.

Lesson 89   Soft g

Vocabulary Words				Sight Words	
age	strange	cottage	college	gentle	circumstance
cage	danger	village	allergy	general	awry
wage	large	package	clergy	giant	oxygen
huge	orange	sausage	pigeon	ginger	purpose
vegetable	baggage	voyage	engine	giraffe	committee
change	cabbage	carriage	magic	germ	dangerous
		garage		suggest	solve

✳ Usually, when the letter 'e' or 'i' comes after the letter 'g', then it sounds like (j).

✳ See Instructions Page 65.

Sentences

1. Do not get too close to that cage! That huge lion could be dangerous if he can reach you with his front claws.

2. What age does a person have to be to work and earn a minimum wage?

3. Mr. Baxter thinks it sure seems strange how the large crate of oranges just disappeared from his front porch.

4. Mrs. Post was informed that there was a change in our travel plans to France; now we are going to stay in a cute little cottage in a French village.

5. Miss Jane put a package of sausage in her baggage.

6. Now let's imagine that we are going on a voyage to a magical land of giants!

7. Are you kidding? Do you really think that an Army general wants his leaders to be gentle when they are training his soldiers?

8. Professor McNutt has decided to call that giraffe, "Ginger," because her spots are the color of the spice, ginger.

9. It is fascinating to hear stories of days long ago, when pigeons would carry messages to people in faraway lands.

10. The engineer is the person who operates the train.

11. In the Cinderella story, the fairy godmother changed the pumpkin into a coach or a carriage.

12. Under the present circumstances, it is impossible to get another oxygen tank down to the deep sea diver because too many things have gone awry.

13. Tom, please explain to us again, what is the purpose of this committee?

14. I know this sounds strange, but Miss Norbat has an allergy to pigeons! When they are very near to her, she develops trouble breathing and needs an oxygen mask to get the problem solved.

Lesson 90   dge, gh, ch

Vocabulary Words				Sight Words
edge	grudge	character	laugh	control
bridge	porridge	rough	machine	convince
budge	ache	tough	parachute	continue
fudge	orchestra	enough		connive
judge	school	cough		contain
				terrible
				wreck

✳ In this lesson, we learn that 'dge' has the sound of (j), 'gh' can have the sound of (f), and 'ch' can have the sound of (k) or the sound of (sh).

✳ In the sight words, 'con' sounds like (kun).

✳ See Instructions Page 65.

Sentences

1. The waters were rough, making it difficult to control the boat while we were fishing with Uncle Stanford.

2. Hank continues to carry a grudge against the judge.

3. Aunt Sydney thinks you have not shown enough tough love to help contain that wild daughter of yours.

4. I just had to laugh when my little boy, Eric, looked up at me with chocolate fudge all over his mouth.

5. Mrs. Clark had to leave work early because she ate fudge for lunch and developed a terrible headache!

6. What is your character like? Are you honest and kind?

7. A person of good character continually tells the truth, is kind and works hard. That person is also dependable.

8. Oh for goodness sake! That girl is standing on the edge of a bridge! She is either a good swimmer or she is crazy!

9. Mother Bear made a large pot of porridge to feed her hungry family, and she did not intend it for Goldilocks.

10. The judge allowed the lawyers to talk endlessly in court.

11. The thief connived his way into the bank vault last evening.

12. The orchestra performed a concert in the park last night.

13. Cousin Jerry is convinced that our radar is picking up the wreckage of an old sunken submarine.

14. I do not want to jump out of an airplane with a parachute. The very thought of it scares me to death!

15. Have you finally invented a machine that can cure cancer?

Lesson 91   ph, unusual s

Vocabulary Words				Sight Words
telephone	elephant	cellophane	sugar	recipe
microphone	gopher	emphasis	sure	clarinet
xylophone	trophy	phantom	measure	vacuum
phrase	nephew	physical	pleasure	prevention
phonics	photo	orphan	issue	Ariana
			tissue	

✳ The letters 'ph' sound like (f).

✳ When a word begins with an (x), it sounds like a (z).

✳ The 's' in some words sounds like (sh). For example: "sugar" and "sure."

✳ When used at the end of a word, the letters 'sure' sound like (zhur). For example: "measure."

✳ See Instructions Page 65.

Sentences

1. If you want the crowd to hear you, be sure to use the microphone.

2. Have you ever played a tune on a xylophone?

3. The recipe says to measure the sugar carefully.

4. It is a pleasure to meet you, Miss Ariana.

5. My grandmother told me that when the vacuum was first invented, the machine was called an electric sweeper.

6. My family members are musical. Dad plays a clarinet, Mom plays a violin, Paul and David play the trumpet, Sharon, George and Janice play the piano, Jim plays the guitar, and we all sing.

7. I had my children learn to play the piano because I think learning to read and playing music helps with math reasoning.

8. Did you know that the plural of wolf is wolves? Plural means more than one. You win the grammar trophy!

9. The sweet lady read a silly story about an elephant who loved to talk on the telephone to his friend, the gopher.

10. Have you heard the phrase, "A bit of advice is always nice?"

11. Let's wrap the meat in cellophane and put it in the fridge.

12. Make sure the children practice their phonics lessons.

13. When my friend's parents died, he became an orphan.

14. The phantom jet is above the clouds; we just can't see it.

15. Let's take our photo album to school to show our friends.

16. The principal emphasized that we should not be tardy.

Lesson 92   igh aigh eigh ough augh

Vocabulary Words				Sight Words
high	tight	taught	eighty	sign
fight	bright	daughter	freight	bouquet
light	fright	naughty	eighth	jewelry
might	bought	weigh	straight	diamond
night	fought	sleigh	bough	
right	brought	neighbor	though	
sight	caught	eight	through	

✶ In these words, the letters 'gh' are silent.

✶ See Instructions Page 65.

Sentences

1. Mr. Wilkins bought his daughter a beautiful, purple sweater for her eighth birthday. She was simply delighted.

2. My naughty younger brothers have fought every day since I can remember! The neighbors got used to the yelling.

3. Steven brought his girlfriend a bouquet of flowers on Valentine's Day, and you should have seen her blush!

4. Clifford is pretty sure that the police caught the thieves in the act of stealing the jewelry at the Diamond Center.

5. The teachers at Elsinore Elementary School taught the students how to read, write and calculate math problems.

6. Even though Sam ate a lot of food, he still didn't weigh as much as others, considering his age and size.

7. When the freight train went through the tunnel, everything was dark and I couldn't see anything until it came out into the light.

8. One of the main branches of a tree is called a bough.

9. Have you ever ridden on a sleigh pulled through the snow by a horse? That is what the song "Jingle Bells" is all about.

10. The neighbors to the right of our home have eight children.

11. You had better hold on tightly because that scary ride will give you a fright. It's not a bright idea to go on it.

12. Drive straight ahead for what seems like an eternity, until you catch a glimpse of the blue and white sign for the hotel.

13. My eighty-five year old father likes to watch the news every evening. However, tonight will be different. The kids are coming over.

14. August is the eighth month of the year, and it is my favorite because our family usually has weddings in August.

15. The fireworks were a spectacular sight in the summer night's sky!

Lesson 93   Silent Letters   l b

Vocabulary Words				Sight Words
calf	yolk	stalk	crumb	science
half	walk	lamb	thumb	scientist
salmon	talk	limb	climb	design
folk	chalk	comb		Samantha

✱ In the first group of words, the letter 'l' is silent. For example: "calf" sounds like (caf) and "walk" sounds like (wok).

✱ In the second group of words, the letter 'b' is silent. For example: "lamb" sounds like (lam).

✱ See Instructions Page 65.

Sentences

1. When the calf grows up, will it be a cow or a bull?

2. Bill and Jane caught a large salmon. They will cut it in half in order to share it.

3. Let's walk while we talk so we can get to the meeting in time.

4. I find it interesting that celery grows on a stalk.

5. The yolk in the middle of the chicken egg is dark yellow.

6. Jake's cat loves to climb upon that limb to watch birds.

7. Felix, bring me a comb so I can comb your hair.

8. Why don't you pull that plate closer, to catch the crumbs?

9. Shawna still sucks her thumb at ten years of age!

10. Dan's favorite subject is science, and when he grows up he wants to become a scientist.

11. Although Samantha is still a beginning artist, she drew an amazing design.

12. My wife's folks are coming over for dinner tonight.

13. Although I recently bought you a box of white chalk, you don't seem to have any now. What's going on, Patty?

14. School classrooms used to have huge black or green chalkboards for teachers to write on. Now they have white boards and use dry erase markers.

15. When my dad taught me how to make waffles, he showed me how to separate the egg yolk from the egg whites.

Lesson 94   Silent Letters k t

Vocabulary Words				Sight Words
knee	knock	often	castle	adjective
knew	know	soften	whistle	earth
knife	known	fasten	Christmas	nursery
			chestnut	Devon

✴ In the first group of words the letter 'k' is silent.

✴ In the second group of words the letter 't' is silent.

✴ See Instructions Page 65.

Sentences

1. Now listen to me, I don't know what you've heard, but there's no way on earth I will let you go there by yourself.

2. Dad's knee was damaged again during a football game, and he's afraid that a doctor will suggest surgery.

3. We must be careful when cutting vegetables with a knife.

4. An adjective is a word that gives information about nouns. It can describe, tell how many, tell which one and it can tell whose.

5. Listen carefully to this sentence and tell me which words are the adjectives. "The clear, brown table is set for dinner."

6. Who is that knocking? Carissa, please go answer the door.

7. Rebecca often asks Andrew to fasten her necklace for her.

8. The king and queen live in a castle in their kingdom.

9. During Christmas season, people sing a song about roasting chestnuts on an open fire.

10. When Uncle Devon whistles a happy tune, it causes me to smile.

11. You need to soften your voice when entering the baby's nursery, because she may be sleeping.

12. I know that you know how to use a computer, but I still want to explain some things to you.

13. Dad, I heard a strange noise again coming from the rooftop.

14. The planet we live on is called Earth. I like it here.

15. Ah ha! I knew you would be back asking for help!

16. If you climb out too far on that limb, it may break off!

Lesson 95   Silent Letter w

Vocabulary Words				Sight Words
wrap	wrench	wrote	two	experience
wren	wretch	whole	sword	extra
wreck	write	whose	answer	once
				rhythm

✳ In these words, the letter 'w' is silent.

✳ See Instructions Page 65.

Sentences

1. Everyone needs to learn how to wrap a present, and these women know how to teach you.

2. Do you see that lovely wren? It is flying toward the jungles.

3. Please answer me this: whose backpack was left on my front porch? Is it an extra one that no one needs?

4. Justin is not ashamed to admit that he ate the whole cherry pie! I witnessed the feast myself!

5. The teacher told the class, "I want you to write two complete sentences about the legendary King Arthur and his sword."

6. Once upon a time, my father wrote a book about his harrowing experiences during World War II, when he was an enlisted man in the Navy.

7. Mr. Johnson's dog, Dutchess, is absolutely amazing. She can outrun and outhunt any hound I've ever seen.

8. Unless Mrs. White is given a different assignment by noon, she plans to sign up as a volunteer at the Senior Center to help prepare the Christmas banquet and party.

9. It's about time for Judy to shake up the salad and add the tomatoes, avocados and dressing. Dinner is almost ready.

10. Can you feel the rhythm of the beat that Perry is playing on the piano? Let's dance to the beat.

11. Once in a while I probably frustrate poor Bobby because it takes me so long to put my make-up on in the morning.

12. What does Tim think the process should be for developing this film in his new dark room?

13. Jennifer checked the toolbox in the garage and she couldn't find the wrench.

14. What she did find, though, was a hammer, screwdrivers, nuts, bolts and nails.

Lesson 96   Silent Letters h d c p s n

Vocabulary Words			Sight Words
honest	Wednesday	cupboard	type
hour	handsome	raspberry	typical
rhyme	handkerchief	island	observe
	scene	autumn	drawer
	scissors	column	Georgia

✳ In this lesson, each of the Vocabulary Words has a silent letter.

✳ See Instructions Page 65.

Sentences

1. On Wednesday of last week, my husband and I were at the Grand Canyon, early in the morning, enjoying the magnificent scene of the sun rising over the canyon.

2. Mrs. Galloway told me that in her opinion, our son, Eric, has grown up into such a fine, handsome young man.

3. Please don't make a major issue about it; just go get me the scissors so that I can trim the hair over your ears.

4. In days long ago, when paper tissues weren't readily available, men and women carried handkerchieves with them in their pocket or purse.

5. I want you to be absolutely honest with me; did you take the money that was lying on my dresser drawer?

6. In order for our nephew, Tom, to make tomorrow's early morning flight in time, what hour must we wake him up?

7. The children and I like to play word games, such as choosing a word and rhyming with it.

8. For example, these words all rhyme: men, ten, pen, hen, den, Ken, Ben and Jen.

9. I asked Henry if he would get the raspberry jelly in the top cupboard for me, and he refused!

10. On our family vacation this autumn, all of my relatives will be going to a small island off Georgia.

11. The teacher told us to write all our spelling words in one column, not two.

12. The Army soldiers invaded the island by moonlight.

13. Mr. Jersey's nephew is a fine example of a typical Army soldier.

14. I have observed, that the type of stories I love begin with "Once upon a time."

15. The island has its own unique type of raspberries growing wildly in the hills.

Lesson 97   tion sion cian

Vocabulary Words				Sight Words
action	auction	description	attention	patient
nation	caution	revolution	mention	economy
station	position	constitution	mansion	graduate
direction	fiction	punctuation	conclusion	duplicate
fraction	notion	situation	impression	separate
solution	lotion	nutrition	division	intricate
condition	vacation	vibration	musician	stadium

✳ In this lesson, we learn that word endings, 'tion', 'sion' and 'cian' sound like (shun) or (zhun) as in "division."

✳ See Instructions Page 65.

Sentences

1. Please take caution while driving to the train station because there will be lots of people not paying attention.

2. On what basis did you get the notion that Fred's story was fiction instead of biographical?

3. Did I hear that you gave a description of the bank robber?

4. Dr. Jacobson mentioned that nutrition plays the most important role in developing a healthy body.

5. Aunt Helen gave us directions to the auction on Saturday.

6. The reason for the people's revolution is that they want a new constitution in order to guarantee certain freedoms.

7. The situation was horrible; men, women and children were fleeing for their lives, with no solution in sight.

8. When I grow up I want to be a musician and be able to play several different musical instruments.

9. If you want to be an effective leader, you'll need to learn when to take action and when to be patient.

10. My goodness, the music was so loud at the graduation that we could feel the vibrations all the way across the stadium!

11. The old man had been a fugitive from the law for thirty years, but he notified the police that if his conditions were met, he would turn himself in, and he did!

12. When it comes to math, my favorite activity is division.

13. When we exercise, it is important to position our bodies correctly.

14. It is my impression that our nation's economy is in trouble.

15. The cost is now a fraction of what it used to be.

Lesson 98 ture

Vocabulary Words				Sight Words
pasture	future	venture	adventure	assignment
picture	fixture	moisture	temperature	area
nature	mixture	overture	miniature	geology
			furniture	quiet
				humidity
				Beethoven

✳ In this lesson, we learn that 'ture' sounds like (chur).

✳ See Instructions Page 65.

Sentences

1. The best milk comes from cows that go out to pasture regularly, the way nature intended for them.

2. The art teacher says that our assignment for tonight is to paint a picture of a nature scene, including sky and land.

3. Grandma is worried and doesn't think we should venture out into the storm tonight. Let's stay home and play it safe.

4. Did you notice that our parents are convinced that Samantha has a bright future ahead of her in the area of geology?

5. Mr. Jackman started his own business. He carves and sells miniature furniture. He uses wood from the finest oak trees.

6. You can understand that Sandra's feelings are a mixture of excitement and anticipation, awaiting her soon coming wedding day.

7. At the concert, the Philharmonic orchestra played a beautiful piece called an overture, composed by Beethoven.

8. Paul and his high school buddies had hysterical adventures they will remember forever. You'll laugh as he retells their antics.

9. Mr. Clayton explained to me that a fixture is something that is attached or fixed to the house, such as a bathtub or a sink.

10. If it is one's nature to be that way, or do something that way, then we say it is natural for them. It is natural for Twyla to sing in the shower. She simply can't remain quiet.

11. Is it natural, or normal for this class of boys to be so quiet or do you think it's because this assignment is so fascinating?

12. Oh no, I'm afraid that the temperature will be rising above 100 degrees again today.

13. Can you feel the moisture in the air after the rain has stopped? The moisture in the air is called humidity.

14. I read in the newspaper that some scientists say the earth is getting warmer each year. Is this true?

15. After Hollister graduates, make sure she makes a duplicate of her diploma. She'll need it to get into graduate school.

Lesson 99 tious cious ous eous

Vocabulary Words				Sight Words
fictitious	humongous	ambiguous	famous	Cheyenne
nutritious	horrendous	fabulous	jealous	Cherokee
vicious	monstrous	continuous	various	Apache
righteous	dangerous	numerous		Guinness
gorgeous	pompous	ludicrous		restaurant
				La Vonne
				Charlotte

✱ The endings 'tious' and 'cious' sound like (shus).

✱ The endings 'ous' and 'eous' sounds like (us).

✱ See Instructions Page 65.

Sentences

1. I believe that Mrs. LaVonne is truly a righteous young lady.

2. I wouldn't say that Cynthia is gorgeous, but she sure is pretty!

3. Since that story is not a true story, we would say that it is a fictitious story, or we can just call it fiction.

4. Most of the times, Mother makes very nutritious meals for us, but sometimes, we go out for junk food at fast food restaurants.

5. Daniel wonders if someday he will be famous and everyone will know about him.

6. The accident in the fog involved so many vehicles that it was a horrendous mess.

7. The homework Mrs. Moore assigns in honors English class is continuous; there seems to be no end in sight!

8. Could you tell that Hazel was jealous of the attention that Charlotte was getting from Vince?

9. Cheyenne said she heard about some people back east who made a humongous cheesecake, hoping to get into the Guinness Book of World Records.

10. Cindy loves so many various types of desserts, that she can't decide on any one as a favorite.

11. When we study American history, we learn that there are so many different Native American tribes, such as Apache, Cherokee and Cheyenne.

12. In the movie there was a monstrous creature that scared us so badly that we screamed.

13. The dog that attacked Mrs. Blakemore was vicious and had to be taken away.

Lesson 100 tial cial tient cient tual

Vocabulary Words				Sight Words
special	facial	spatial	effectual	fiasco
especially	beneficial	efficient	factual	Rodriguez
superficial	crucial	patient	punctual	psychology
financial	palatial	quotient	conceptual	sociology
				archeology
				catalog
				synagogue
				idealogue

✳ In this lesson, we learn that 'tial' and 'cial' sound like (shul) or (chul).

✳ 'tient' and 'cient' sound like (shunt) or (shint).

✳ 'tual' sounds like (shoowel) as in "effectual."

✳ See Instructions Page 65.

When done with this lesson:

✳ Praise/encourage student! **"YOU HAVE DONE IT! You have worked so hard! I am so proud of you! You are a fantastic reader!"**

✳ Time to Celebrate!!

Sentences

1. Isabella is looking for a special, formal red dress to wear at the upcoming Valentine's Banquet.

2. Mrs. Rodriguez specializes in baking fancy, multiple layer wedding cakes.

3. Mr. Henderson is frustrated with the demands of his boss, and it shows in his facial expressions.

4. Anthony was expecting a financial gain by taking the position at the other company, but now he's not so sure it was worth it.

5. My family is not rich. Once I saw a house that looked like the palace of a king and queen. It was palatial!

6. If you look at the problem in a superficial manner, it will seem one way; but if you take a deeper, more analytical look, you may come up with a different opinion.

7. Dr. McNutt was always punctual when arriving to his economics class. His lectures were so factual his students kept taking notes.

8. Geometry is the study of spatial relationships.

9. The class was instructed to conceptualize what society would be like if all people followed the teachings of Scripture.

10. The night before the exam, it was very beneficial for me to review what I had learned in class that semester.

11. It is important to be efficient with your time when attending college and holding a job simultaneously.

12. Archaeology is a fascinating field of study. It is the scientific study of historic peoples and their cultures by analysis of their artifacts.

13. The new patient in that ward keeps saying he is a psychology or sociology professor at the university in Massachusetts.

14. I learned another math term today, a "quotient" is the answer to a division problem.

15. It was such a fiasco when our dog, Rodriquez, found a vacuum bag filled with dirt and dust in the trash bin, and shook it to pieces inside the house!

The following sections are not part of the reading program. You may read these sections and implement some or all of the material if you find the material to be helpful. The author designed these sections to be helpful in developing some of the skills that your student will need to learn to be successful in school. This section was not meant to be exhaustive, for there are books written on these subjects. These sections are intended to supplement the reading program as an added benefit to the reader and teacher.

Optional Activities

Important Note: *When working with a very young reader, do not worry about reading comprehension, spelling or writing development. Just concentrate on learning how to read and building a child's vocabulary. As a reader gains skill and confidence, you can add the following activities.*

Vocabulary Building

Here are some ideas that will support your child's vocabulary development:

Infant

Infants learn language incredibly quickly by hearing people speak. Long before a child actually talks, he has been listening and learning. Therefore, you can help your child learn to speak correctly, by speaking correctly yourself. Your child will learn to understand and speak the words you use around him. Therefore, don't feel that it is necessary to talk in simple words to a baby or child. Just talk naturally. If you use big, adult-like words, your child will learn to use and understand big words. Often times, a person is considered to be more intelligent because of the words he uses in speaking and writing. Talk to your baby often. Whether you are busy or relaxing, talk to the baby about anything and everything. Continue this as the child is growing up. Explain where you are going, what you are going to do and what is happening. This will accomplish several wonderful things such as: 1. Your child will understand more about life. 2. Your child will have a better relationship with you. 3. Your child will be able to communicate better. 4. Your child will do better in school because of his increased understanding and ability to communicate, and 5. Your child will have a larger vocabulary.

Ages 2-5

Use the words that your child can read from the lessons, in daily conversation with your child when it is reasonable to do so. Point out the words when they come up in everyday life. As new words enter your conversations with your child, be sure to explain the meaning of the words. Research shows that a child's vocabulary will greatly enhance learning and achievement in school.

Age 6+

When your child learns the meaning of a new word, have him write it on an index card. These words can be practiced as flash cards.

Reading Comprehension

Reading comprehension simply means that a person understands what he or she reads.

A person will comprehend what he or she reads if the following **three requirements are met:**

Requirement 1   The child knows the meaning of the words that are being read. That means the child already hears and possibly uses the words being read, **or** is being taught what the new words mean.

Requirement 2   The child can read fast enough for the words to make sense together. In other words, if a child is taking a long time figuring out what each word says, then he won't be able to understand the sentence.

Requirement 3   The child is relaxed enough and wants to think about what he is reading. Here are three examples of when a child may not be in the right mindset to think about what he is reading: 1) a child is stressing out about making mistakes, 2) a child is reading on auto pilot while daydreaming about something else, or 3) a child is REQUIRED to read something that she finds boring, and she might not be paying attention to the content.

How do we check for a student's comprehension? Talk with your student about what she has read. Ask questions to find out if your child understands. Discussing the content will enhance your child's thinking skills. Don't stress out about this. Just talk about the sentences. It will come naturally.

At the end of a lesson, you can ask your child questions that relate to the sentences that she has just read. Ask one question at a time and give the child time to answer the question. You can ask different questions for each lesson, because the sentences are different. Here are some sample questions that can get you started:

Sample comprehension questions <u>for sentences</u> in this book:
> ➤ Who was in this sentence?
> ➤ What happened in the sentence?
> ➤ Why was the boy upset?

You can also check for reading comprehension after you read other books or stories to your child or when your child reads other books or stories. Ask one question at a time and give the child time to answer the question. You can ask different questions for each story. Here are some sample questions that can get you started:

248

Sample comprehension questions <u>for other books or stories:</u> These often are questions about Who, What, When, Where, Why and How.

➤ Tell me the name of someone in the story. (Who)
➤ Tell me what happened in the story. (What)
➤ When did it happen? (When)
➤ Where did this story take place? (Where)
➤ Why did _____ happen? (Why)
➤ How did the problem get solved? (How)
➤ How did the story end? (How)

Writing Development

It is good to let your child hold a crayon to use for coloring or scribbling at a very young age. This activity is good for many reasons and should be encouraged. When the child is older and you feel he or she can handle a pencil safely, then you can exchange the crayon for a pencil. When the child is 3 or 4 years old, show him how to hold the crayon or pencil correctly. It takes practice to hold the pencil properly and needs to be done often. Please find an ABC handwriting chart that shows the proper way to make letters. Show your child the proper way to make letters. Get two pieces of paper and two crayons or pencils. Then sit next to your child and give him one piece of paper and one crayon or pencil. Then, using the ABC chart as a reference, you draw a letter one line at a time while your child watches and copies you on his piece of paper. Then you can make the next line with your child copying you.

When your child can write letters properly, then it is time to start having her write the three-letter words learned in Lesson 1. I think it is best to have a child learn to write the same words she can read. **After** your child has learned to read each lesson, then have your student write the words and sentences. Your child may learn to read, write and spell all at the same time.

After a lesson can be read:

Have the student copy some of the words while saying them.

➤ Have the student copy some of the sentences while reading them.
➤ As the child matures, have him write sentences, and later stories, using the words on the vocabulary list.

NOTE: Generally we start teaching young children to print before we teach a child to write in cursive. Printing can be taught in preschool and kindergarten. Cursive is generally taught in 3rd grade and is considered the normal writing for adults. However, many adults prefer printing. At least try to teach your child to write his signature in cursive.

Warning: Do not start writing and spelling if your student protests strongly. He may stop reading altogether. It's better just to have him learn to read for now. We don't want to push too much. We want reading to be fun!

Spelling

I would not start spelling activities until a child is 4 or 5 years old, unless they are eager to do so earlier.

Once your child can write letters properly, then it is time to start having her learn to spell the same three-letter words that she has learned to read in Lesson 1. It makes sense to have a child learn to spell the same words she can read because spelling uses the same skill of sounding out the letters, and the word pattern is fresh in her mind. Therefore, after your child has learned to read each lesson, have your child write out the Vocabulary Words. You can decide how many words she should write. Choose at least several words from each word pattern in the list. Give the child a pencil or pen and a piece of paper. Close the book or move it so the student cannot see the lesson. Then say, **"I will say a word. Listen to the word and write it down on this piece of paper."** Then say the word, for example "cat". Wait patiently while your child tries to write it out. If your child is unsure how to write the word without looking at it, then tell her to say the word slowly and write the sounds that she hears. For example, exaggerate the word "cat" so that she can hear the "c" "a" and "t".

Summary:

After each lesson can be read easily:
1. With the book open for the student to see:
  ➤ **Have student copy the words while saying them.**
  ➤ **Have student copy the sentences while reading them.**
2. Do not let the student see the lesson for these activities:
  ➤ **Say the words to the student and have him or her write the words.**
  ➤ **Say the sentences from the lesson to the student and have him or her write the sentences.**

Spelling may come easily when the student is spelling the same words that she has just learned to read. If spelling does not come easily for your child, here are some study tips: **Have your child...**
1. Look at the word and say it.
2. Spell the word out loud while looking at it.
3. Cover the word and spell it out loud while writing it.
4. Look at the book and check to see if you spelled the word correctly.
   ➤ If the word is not spelled correctly, then start over again with number 1 above. Keep practicing!

Warning: Do not start writing and spelling if the student protests strongly. He may stop reading altogether. It's better just to have him learn to read for now. We want reading to be fun!

Reading Standards

What follows is a list of the reading standards that are to be taught in schools in the State of California. Presently, each state has its own list, however, there is presently an effort being made to compile a national list for all states. *Ready, Set, Read* addresses each of these standards throughout the course of the reading program.

California Reading Standards

Kindergarten

Concepts About Print

K.1.1 Identify the front cover, back cover, and title page of a book.

K.1.2 Follow words from left-to-right and top-to-bottom on the printed page.

K.1.3 Understand that printed materials provide information.

K.1.4 Recognize that sentences in print are made up of separate words.

K.1.5 Distinguish letters from words.

K.1.6 Recognize and name all uppercase and lowercase letters of the alphabet.

Phonemic Awareness

K.1.7 Track (move sequentially from sound to sound) and represent the number, sameness/difference, and order of two and three isolated phonemes.

K.1.8 Track and represent changes in simple syllables and words with two and three sounds as one sound is added, substituted, omitted, shifted, or repeated.

K.1.9 Blend vowel-consonant sounds orally to make words or syllables.

K.1.10 Identify and produce rhyming word in response to an oral prompt.

K.1.11 Distinguish orally stated one-syllable words and separate into beginning or ending sounds.

K.1.12 Track auditorily each word in a sentence and each syllable in a word.

K.1.13 Count the number of sounds in words.

Decoding and Word Recognition
K.1.14 Match all consonant and short-vowel sounds to appropriate letters.

K.1.15 Read 10 simple one-syllable, high frequency words.

K.1.16 Understand that as letters of words change, so do the sounds.

First Grade

Concepts About Print
1.1.1 Match oral words to printed words.

1.1.2 Identify the title and author of a reading selection

1.1.3 Identify letters, words and sentences.

Phonemic Awareness
1.1.4 Distinguish initial, medial, and final sounds in single-syllable words.

1.1.5 Distinguish long and short vowel sounds in orally stated single-syllable words.

1.1.6 Create and state a series of rhyming words, including consonant blends.

1.1.7 Add, delete or change target sounds to change words.

1.1.8 Blend two to four phonemes into recognizable words.

1.1.9 Segment single-syllable words into their components.

Decoding and Word Recognition
1.1.10 Generate the sounds from all the letters and letter patterns, including consonant blends and long and short vowel patterns, and blend those sounds into recognizable words.

1.1.11 Read common, irregular sight words.

1.1.12 Use knowledge of vowel digraphs and r-controlled letter-sound associations to read words.

1.1.13 Read compound words and contractions.

1.1.14 Read inflectional forms and root words.

1.1.15 Read common word families.

1.1.16 Read aloud with fluency in a manner that sounds like natural speech.

Grade 2

Decoding and Word Recognition
2.1.1 Recognize and use knowledge of spelling patterns when reading.

2.1.2 Apply knowledge of basic syllabication rules when reading.

2.1.3 Decode two-syllable nonsense words and regular multi-syllable words.

2.1.4 Recognize common abbreviations.

2.1.5 Identify and correctly use regular plurals and irregular plurals.

2.1.6 Read aloud with fluency and accuracy, and with appropriate intonation and expression.

Grade 3

Decoding and Word Recognition
3.1.1 Know and use complex word families when reading to decode unfamiliar words.

3.1.2 Decode regular multi-syllable words.

3.1.3 Read aloud narrative and expository text fluently and accurately and with appropriate pacing, intonation and expression.

Grade 4, Grade 5 and Grade 6

Word Recognition
1.1 Read narrative and expository text aloud with grade-appropriate fluency and accuracy and with appropriate pacing, intonation and expression.

Questions & Answers

1. How do I start?

For a baby:
Read "Step 1: For Babies" and use the flash cards to begin teaching your baby the letter sounds. (See Table of Contents for page number)

Young Child:
Go to Step 1 (See Table of Contents for page number)

2. What if my student already reads, but not very well?

➤ Do Steps 1 and 2.

➤ Go to lesson 1 and have your student read just the list of Vocabulary Words and Sight Words. Continue with each of the next lessons, just reading the word lists until your student starts to make mistakes. That is where to stop and begin with that reading lesson.

➤ When in doubt, go through each lesson completely.

3. What if a student struggles with the lesson?

Your student should learn at her own pace. Continue to repeat the same lesson until it is mastered. You should go back to previous lessons to review and build confidence. Do not worry, and tell your student not to worry. Mastery will come with enough practice. If you give up then your student won't learn. People learn better when they feel hope. Your student needs to believe that you think she can do it eventually.

4. What if my child won't cooperate with me?

Try something to motivate your child. I try the "nice" approach first, and I would recommend these in this order:

➤ Tell the child we are going to have fun and learn something new.

➤ Appeal to their ego to get smarter and learn new information.

➤ Offer a reward: treat, fun time, money

And if the "nice" approach does not work, then I get tough (if the child is 5 or older) after all, I AM the parent! When it comes to important things, I require my children to do certain things that I know are good for them. And let's face it, some children are never going to CHOOSE to work. So we try to make it fun. But for some children, we have to give up on the fun and just make them do it. I don't mind waiting twenty years for their "thank you."

Here are some ideas:

254

➤ Offer an incentive: If you read with me for 10 minutes, then we'll...

➤ The child has a choice, read with you or take away something they really like to do or have. Say, **No TV, games or dessert if you won't read with me. It's your choice.**

Parenting Tips

The author is not representing that she is a trained expert in parenting, although she has raised four children. She has included information in this section that includes personal experience and beliefs. You may or may not agree with her personal beliefs and may choose to disregard this entire section.

How to Help Your Child Become Smarter, More Confident and More Content

Some people are simply born brilliant and it's not due to having an enriched environment or superior genetics. Call it luck or God's gift. But most intelligent people have their intelligence developed by having had experiences that have shaped them. I am in the business of shaping and inspiring young, impressionable minds to become great. You can do this too. It's easy and fun. Here are some ideas of what to do. Add to this list as you interact with your child, because no one knows your child like you do!

➤ Talk to your child a lot, starting when he or she is in the womb.

➤ Get on the floor with your child often and play, chase, and wrestle. Have fun and don't be too rough.

➤ Have fun, laugh with your child, joke around. Be positive to each other and about others.

➤ Engage your child in conversation. Don't do all the talking.

➤ Make eye-contact often while talking. (See more about this in the Teaching Tips section.)

➤ Explain things to your child (even before you are sure they can understand, and before they ask).

➤ Express love and admiration to your child.

➤ Have your child help you do things: clean, cook, fold laundry.

➤ Watch an educational program together on TV and talk about it.

➤ While your child is an infant, start counting to them. (Show them a wall calendar and count the days).

➤ Sing the ABC song to your infant. Teach him the ABC Flash Cards.

➤ Read stories to your child every day.

➤ Talk about happy feelings and hurt feelings. Explain how we can hurt people or make them happy by what we say and do.

➤ Continue teaching your child things and **keep the dialogue open** as he grows up.

➤ Teach your child to read before she goes to kindergarten.

➤ After children can read fluently, then have them read good books. I always require my children to be reading, daily, a certain amount from a book **I have selected** and also from something they have selected. This way, I am continuing to educate them through the books I select.

➤ Go to the library regularly.

➤ Have lots of reading materials around the house within reach.

➤ Play games and toys that stimulate thinking, such as puzzles.

➤ Train your young child in morals, and continue as they grow up until they leave home. They are never too young or too old for this.

Teaching/Parenting Tips

➤ Practice making "eye contact," especially with your baby or young child. That means you and the child look into each other's eyes often while talking. If this manner is used regularly, you will have more success holding a child's attention as they grow up.

➤ Making eye contact is very important for several other reasons. I am convinced that a child will feel more important with self-respect if you have regularly looked him in the eyes while speaking to him. I believe that a child will more likely develop a sense of her own identity, self-worth and confidence. A "bonding" or special connection is made between the two of you.

➤ Keep your attitude good about reading. Be excited! You are teaching the most important thing in his educational life! If a child learns to read well, he is more likely to be successful in everything else. No matter what interests him, he will enjoy it more and go farther if he can read well.

➤ Encourage the student. As she takes small steps, make positive comments such as: "Wow, you are doing it!" "You are smart!" "I knew you would learn!" "I love to hear you read!" and "I am proud of you!" If your child is having difficulty, attempt a small amount at a time and do it more times. Give A LOT of encouragement for a small bit of success. We MUST help this child believe that she or he can and will learn to read. Also, WE must believe that the child can learn to read. Our attitude is crucial to the success of our children. If we put them down, or if they sense that we don't think they can do it, they will fail.

➤ Your child may suggest reading to you at different times during the day. He may be excited about reading. He or she may want that special time with you. He or she may want your undivided attention. Give it to them if you can. Encourage their natural desire to learn. Use their desire to be close to you to build that special bond.

➤ Be careful not to cause another child to be jealous. Make special time with the other child also. Each child needs to know that you love each one just as much. If you DO love one more than another, that is unfortunate. DO NOT LET IT SHOW! It will not help anyone to know that, not even the favored child. You will end up being resented by all, including the favored one.

➤ If you are teaching an older child who has already experienced failure, you will have to find a delicate balance between encouraging and pushing. We need to plant hope in the child's mind that they can learn and succeed, and we need to push the child to work and try. You must believe in your student. Every person can learn to read, though they learn at different speeds.

➤ DO NOT SAY mean things to a child such as "You're stupid, why does it take you so long?" or "I didn't think you could do it." People are fragile; they can be damaged or broken. If you rob them of self-worth, they will not be successful. They can carry hurt for the rest of their lives. If you make a mistake and say something horrible, then humbly apologize to try to undo the damage. Say something like, "I am sorry for saying those mean words. It's not true. I guess I'm just too tired right now." "Let's take a break. I need to be more patient." And be quick to say, "I am sorry, please forgive me." When I have made mistakes and said inappropriate things, I have apologized for my words and meant it. The child needs to see you admitting you're wrong and apologizing. It's amazing how sweetly they will forgive you and they will trust you more for showing that you are not perfect.

➤ DO NOT compare a slower learner to a faster one. Different people learn at different speeds. Allow for these differences.

Parent's Mission

As parents, our job is to train and prepare our children for adulthood. That means we must decide what is important to teach them and work towards that goal. Do not expect the schools or churches to do your job. You must have an agenda. Without an agenda, the child will be raised in a haphazard manner, which may have disastrous results.

Write your own Mission Statement. This can be as simple as putting your parenting goals on a piece of paper. Each parent's Mission will look different, reflecting that parent's values. Put some thought into this, for it is more important than most things we do in life. If you have a partner, it would be good to work on this together. If the two of you strongly disagree on what's important, then don't let that stop you from writing your own and using it. This agenda doesn't have to be written. But it should be thoughtfully considered. You might tape it to the refrigerator as a reminder.

Remember, if you don't teach your children your values, then they will learn values from somewhere else. That other place might be the television, or someone with values you perceive as very unfavorable. No doubt you've heard the saying "he got in with the wrong group?" Well, think about it. WHY did he get in with the wrong group? It could be the child was looking for acceptance, or looking for a "cool" identity, or just looking for purpose and meaning in life. It is better to turn off the TV and do things with your child. Talk to him or her. Laugh together and cry together. Explain life and LIVE life together.

I have given you my Mission Statement below as an example:

Here is my agenda for educating my own children:

Major Goals
➤ Love God
➤ Be honest
➤ Be responsible
➤ Be hardworking
➤ Be kind

Minor Goals
- ➤ Behave in a socially appropriate way.
- ➤ Have good manners
- ➤ Teach them whatever I can, that will help them in life:
    - ➤ How to take care of yourself
    - ➤ How to respond to others
    - ➤ How to deal with success
    - ➤ How to cope with challenges
    - ➤ The value of earning money
    - ➤ How to spend and save
    - ➤ How to budget
    - ➤ How to do laundry
    - ➤ How to spend our time wisely
    - ➤ How to plan for the future
    - ➤ What to look for in a mate
    - ➤ How to handle dating
    - ➤ How to cook
    - ➤ What to eat to be healthy
    - ➤ How to treat people
    - ➤ How to treat animals

The way to accomplish your agenda is to talk and share with your child as he or she is growing up. As things happen, explain it. Tell them why things are happening. Tell them why someone is upset or hurt. If you aren't sure "why" something happens, or "why" someone is hurt or angry, then talk about the possible reasons. Talk about what happens when... and the list goes on and on. You have about 18 years, so get started. Don't forget, you can always ask others for help.

Warning: TV, Movies, Video Games, Computer

You will have more success holding a child's (or adult's) attention for teaching and telling them ANYTHING if he is not regularly watching a lot of TV. Here's why. TV and movies, video games, and the Internet can have a lot of action, color and noise. If a person is used to a lot of stimulation like this, then listening to a person tell you something seems pretty boring and he may not continue to focus on what is being said. This is true whether you are listening to anyone, including a parent, teacher or preacher. So think about it. If you allow your child to watch a lot of TV or movies or play video games or surf the Internet, you may be setting him up to have poor attention span and to do poorly in school. I know there may be benefits to doing these activities SOMETIMES, but limit it.

➤ **TV, Movies.** Watching TV and movies is a passive activity. People tend to get lazy, less creative and EAT MORE. Watching commercials tends to make people want MORE THINGS. People tend to become more dissatisfied with what they have and WHO they have. I raised my children with very little TV. I told them, "Let's not watch others live, let's live ourselves." About commercials I said, "Do you see how they are trying to get us to buy things?" Ask questions to help your child develop the ability to think critically. Make comments on what happens in the show. Point out bad attitudes, horrible choices and wrong actions. Talk and warn them about where such behavior could lead. Teach morals. If you don't, they will learn from someone else or the show itself, and it may not be what you want them to learn. Remember, the purpose of shows are to make someone money. They are not necessarily realistic, or wholesome; therefore, you need to be talking about it. If the show has good values and attitudes, make good comments which will show your child that you approve.

Family Time

Talk and laugh with your family. Play indoor and outdoor games with the kids. Teach them how to do things. Do household chores, gardening, cooking. Do projects together such as fixing something. Take walks, ride bikes or read a book. There are great things to do with your time to promote healthy family life!

Answer Key

Lessons	Sentence #
1. The man is Dan.	(#5)
2. The rat sat on the bat. The rat is on the bat	(#11 & 15)
3. The cat and rat are mad.	(#8)
4. I can tag Dan and Nan.	(#5)
5. Dan and Dad have maps and caps.	(#13)
6. Nan went bam! bam! on Sam's van.	(#14)
7. Will Tab nab Dad's hat?	(#4)
8. Sal put Max's sax in the vat of wax!	(#14)
9. Dad lit the wick on the wax.	(#6)
10. Max has two fins.	(#3)
11. Dan can put a wig on his pig.	(#8)
12. The kid hid the pan and the lid.	(#10)
13. Do not tip the can, Al!	(#10)
14. Are you about to get into the pen with the two hens?	(#13)
15. The hen has begun to play with the hog.	(#12)
16. Why did she put the pet in the net?	(#5)
17. I could sop it up with a mop if you would let me.	(#15)
18. I want the ox to do his job and lug that box of logs.	(#12)
19. There is a gull up there in the fog.	(#12)
20. Sal, do not kick that dog or he will get mad!	(#10)
21. Mom wants to rest, and then she will dust.	(#5)
22. Our band is not just any band. It is the best band in the land!	(#8)
23. That elf in the act was a bit daft when he kept yelping.	(#9)
24. I don't think Rick is too fond of frogs and crabs.	(#12)
25. Glen thinks we should go slop the hogs with Brent.	(#8)
26. Hal crammed the stumps of logs he cut down into the back of the van.	(#12)
27. Down the block we could see the boys pressing against the glass of the store.	(#10)
28. The kids hung around; they like to play ping pong.	(#4)
29. I can see that Bob's skunk has drunk all of Bob's milk.	(#3)

261

Lessons		Sentence #
30.	Couldn't Rick fix the flat on his truck?	(#14)
31.	Look at all those people. I know they're happy.	(#1)
32.	Hey boys, shall we dash to the shed and brush the dogs?	(#6)
33.	Mrs. Smith thinks Beth is going to cry if she gets stung.	(#3)
34.	Will you please let me pick up the baby chick?	(#13)
35.	That's a very good sketch you did of Miss Hull.	(#10)
36.	Yesterday we worked more on the patch quilt we are making for grandmother.	(#12)
37.	Mom asked you to sweep the rug; why do you sit and weep?	(#14)
38.	The seals are eager to eat fresh fish from the sea.	(#9)
39.	In the meantime, Miss Reed will shoot the hoops.	(#2)
40.	I would love to have a yummy cookie while I sit at home and read a good book.	(#2)
41.	Who dropped the glass lamp on his food?	(#18)
42.	Mom presses the flowers between book pages.	(#11)
43.	Oh wow! The well they drilled is really a gusher!	(#14)
44.	Our mother cat had a litter of baby kittens in September.	(#15)
45.	I got sick from being on the ship out at sea for three days.	(#5)
46.	How swift is the water in the river moving?	(#8)
47.	My Mother always sang me a lullaby before I went to bed.	(#4)
48.	Grandmother uses a lovely linen cloth at dinner time.	(#10)
49.	My grandfather is a humble old man who trembles as he carries his bundle of wood to the woodshed.	(#6)
50.	Uncle Paul says that some camels have one hump on their backs and others have two humps.	(#12)
51.	The Smiths' horse is going to pull that wagon-load of melons from their ranch to the store.	(#1)
52.	Oh Dad, can our family have a picnic at the beach today?	(#4)
53.	My Aunt Katie loves to bake cakes and muffins, and she always puts a cupful of creamy milk in the batter.	(#2)
54.	Hey Mom, toss me the pail so I can bail out the boat!	(#6)
55.	Every night that gray dog bays at the moon for an hour.	(#10)
56.	Hey Joan, why don't we get out of the boat and float on our backs in the cool water?	(#14)

Lessons	Sentence #
57. The tall gray house is casting a shadow across the snow.	(#4)
58. Hey Mack, we heard that you caught a fantastic trout over there in the mountain stream!	(#15)
59. Does the farmer have enough strength to pull that sow out of the deep mud?	(#15)
60. Paul always likes to drink his sun tea with a long straw.	(#3)
61. Don't let your horse eat leaves from the oleander bush for it is poisonous to horses!	(#4)
62. Uncle Bob loves to tell us of his many travels to the jungles of Africa.	(#7)
63. Is that a monkey I see in the tree? I didn't think they lived around here. I thought they were just in zoos.	(#13)
64. If we don't hurry and do something drastic, I'm afraid the bugs will destroy our crops very quickly.	(#3)
65. Since the new dress does not fit Lee well, she is planning to return it to the store pretty soon.	(#12)
66. Let's chase that man and grab his black cape.	(#9)
67. Don't get near that beehive, or you might get stung.	(#11)
68. The water hose broke on my mom's old, battered car. Mom is very upset about it.	(#6)
69. When I grow up I want to play a flute like my Uncle Joe.	(#10)
70. I am sure that Jake was born in Oregon blowing his horn.	(#15)
71. It is time to go to the barber to get your hair cut.	(#10)
72. We should each wash our hands often, to help us not to get sick.	(#7)
73. I can confirm that I have been wearing a girdle for thirteen years!	(#5)
74. Have you ever churned the cream to make butter?	(#14)
75. Little Mackenzie enjoys watching caterpillars crawl on her hand.	(#11)
76. Chet told us about the roaring lion he saw at the zoo.	(#16)
77. That big brown bear has a broad shoulder span.	(#1)
78. Uncle Jay happens to be buried in work this week.	(#16)
79. Sometimes I need to push my son, Dan, to get him to complete his chores. But he is always eager to eat.	(#16)
80. When I was a student, I learned that a canoe is a long narrow boat made out of a hollow tree trunk.	(#11)
81. Dad plans to build a house with the help of his brothers.	(#13)

Lessons	Sentence #
82. Son, I am proud of you for working hard this past month. Your paycheck will be bigger this month because you worked so hard.	(#2)
83. I am truly afraid that there is an alligator in our back pond; don't anyone go back there!	(#5)
84. I think it's cruel how you caught that poor moose!	(#14)
85. Please don't go near that lion behind the bars. He is isolated because he is wild and crazy.	(#9)
86. Julie told me that it's cold only in her classroom.	(#1)
87. Uh oh, it smells like Granny is making her famous vegetable soup which none of us like.	(#7)
88. Grandma almost lost her balance while climbing the stairs!	(#14)
89. Now let's imagine that we are going on a voyage to a magical land of giants!	(#6)
90. I do not want to jump out of an airplane with a parachute. The very thought of it scares me to death.	(#14)
91. The sweet lady read a silly story about an elephant who loved to talk on the telephone to his friend, the gopher.	(#9)
92. The fireworks were a spectacular sight in the summer night's sky.	(#15)
93. Jake's cat loves to climb upon that limb to watch birds.	(#6)
94. If you climb out too far on that limb, it may break off!	(#16)
95. Justin is not ashamed to admit that he ate the whole cherry pie! I witnessed the feast myself!	(#4)
96. The Army soldiers invaded the island by moonlight.	(#12)
97. When I grow up I want to be a musician and be able to play several different musical instruments.	(#8)
98. Oh no, I'm afraid that the temperature will be rising above 100 degrees again today.	(#12)
99. The accident in the fog involved so many vehicles that it was a horrendous mess.	(#6)
100. It was such a fiasco when our dog, Rodriguez, found a vacuum bag filled with dirt and dust in the trash bin, and shook it to pieces inside the house!	(#15)

What Others Are Saying

"Ready, Set, Read is a proven program that taps into a toddler's natural curiosity and desire to learn. In my profession, I've seen that, invariably, college students who love to read are successful in whatever field they choose to study. Therefore, I recommend an early start on reading with Ready, Set, Read."

~Linda Linzey, Ph.D., Assistant Professor, Department of
English and Foreign Languages, Southeastern University

"While other programs move too quickly, Ready, Set, Read includes small, sequential steps to teaching reading – which is perfect for teaching early or struggling readers."

~Melinda Pierson, Ph.D., Chair, Department of Special Education,
California State University, Fullerton

"Because of this wonderful phonics-based program, my daughter now loves reading and cannot get enough of it."

~Kim Grove, mother of a kindergartener

"My daughter loves opening her reading lesson book and practicing her sentences. She will even sit down and open the book and read the sentences to herself."

~Tene, mother of a 3 year old

"I have been using your reading book with my son and have found it very easy and fun to use. My son is now reading sentences, which is very exciting!

~Rosana, mother of a 6 year old

Vera Clark is an outstanding teacher. The results we have seen with her students with learning challenges are impressive.

~Daniel Paquette, Principal

When people see how easy it is to teach someone to read with this simple method, everyone will start doing it. Student's grades will improve. Children will enjoy school more.

~Debbie Garcia, Home Educator

This is amazing! Vera Clark's reading program is so simple and yet so complete. If children learn to read earlier at home they will be confident and more prepared for school.
　　　　　~Karen Jones, first grade Teacher

Just what we've been waiting for. Now anyone can teach someone to read. I look forward to seeing the impact this will have on our children, their grades, self-esteem and ultimately our schools.
　　　　　~Nancy Garcia, Asst. Principal

Practical. Easy to follow. Down to earth. It's a winner.
　　　　　~Hugh Swanke, High School Teacher

I think that down deep we all know that parents should be the primary teacher in a child's life. Mrs. Clark has just given us the material and simple instructions to enable us to be just that.
　　　　　~Richard Kasa, Special Education Teacher

This is perfect! Why didn't someone do this before? Thank you, Vera Clark for putting this in a format we can all understand and use. Future generations will thank you.
　　　　　~Kathy Cottrell, Grandmother, Hydrotherapist

Vera's no-nonsense approach is refreshing. She taught my son, and his improvement was great.
　　　　　~Mike Malan, Father, Electrician

It's all here! All the tools you need to teach someone to read, from beginning to fluency. And Ms. Clark made it so easy!
　　　　　~Dan Roath, Teacher

It's about time someone gave parents the tools to teach their children. Reading is the basic foundation for education. We should teach our children to read before first grade.
　　　　　~Deborah Hite, Educational Advocate for Parents

Vera Clark has given a gift to the people, which empowers families to take charge of their child's education.
　　　　　~Margaret Stoddard, Labor Commissioner (ret.)

Does someone you know read poorly? This step-by-step program will greatly improve their reading. A tremendous remedial tool!
　　　　　~Rosie Goss Hitt, Elementary School Teacher

Vera Clark's down-to-earth approach is refreshing. She writes in "easy listening" language. This method works. I have used it with her for years in the classroom.
　　　　　~Juanita Price, Instructional Aide

Cc

Aa

Dd

Bb

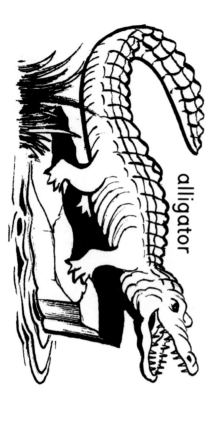

alligator

cat

bear

dog

Gg

Ee

Hh

Ff

gorilla

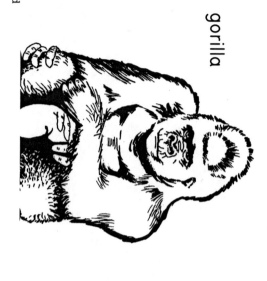

elephant

horse

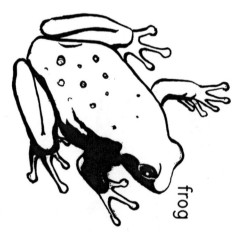

frog

Kk

Īī

L

ジ

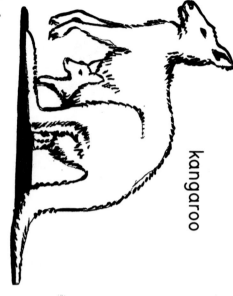

kangaroo

iguana

lion

jaguar

Oo	Mm
Pp	Nn

ostrich

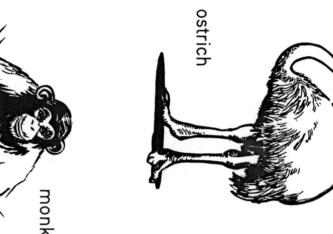

monkey

penguin

nest

Ss

Qq

Tt

Rr

seal

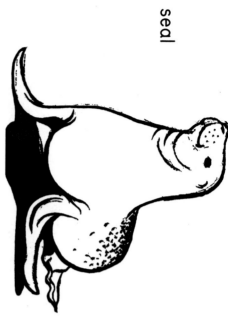

quail

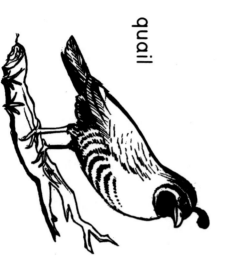

tiger

rhinoceros

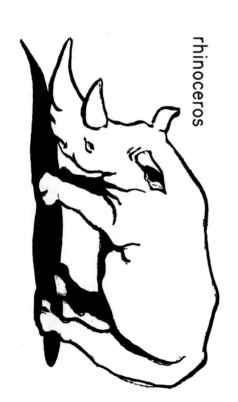

Ww	Uu
Xx	Vv

whale

umbrella

fox

vulture

Yy

Zz

yoyo

zebra

Breinigsville, PA USA
01 October 2010
246471BV00002B/1/P